ONE FLEW OVER THE CHURCH SPIRE

One Flew Over the Church Spire

DAVE SEYMOUR

MINSTREL
Eastbourne

Front cover design by Mike Kazybrid

British Library Cataloguing in Publication Data

Seymour, Dave
   One flew over the church spire.
   I. Title
   822.914

   ISBN 1–85424–116–8

Printed in Great Britain for
Minstrel, an imprint of Monarch Publications Ltd
1 St Anne's Road, Eastbourne, E Sussex BN21 3UN by
Richard Clay Ltd, Bungay, Suffolk
Typeset by J&L Composition Ltd, Filey, North Yorkshire

Foreword

I am very happy to write a foreword to this book which has been written by a man who has very obvious gifts in the field of drama. Dave Seymour has for many years believed that Christian communication needs to be enlivened by modern ways of presenting Christian truth. I too share this concern. Important though proclamation is by the preached word there needs to be visual as well as dramatic forms of communication which can bring home to our audiences the unsearchable riches of Christ. *One Flew Over the Church Spire* is a collection of drama sketches which illustrate Christian principles in a topical and entertaining manner. This is the kind of book that can be used in schools as well as in churches and I wish it great success.

George Carey

Performing Licence

To assist amateur and non-profit-making organisations
no licence fee is necessary for the performance of the
sketches in this book.

However, the waiving of the performance fee does
not allow any organisation to photocopy any of the text
(see copyright notice on page 4).

Professional and profit-making groups wishing to
perform any or all of the sketches in the book should
contact the author for a licence at the address below.

Dave Seymour
PO BOX 1203
Bath
BA1 3TJ

Preface

One Flew Over the Church Spire has been written with a view to introducing a new form of alive and identifiable drama to Christian and educational circles.

The eighteen sketches you'll find inside are designed to convey Christian and biblical principles to a wide audience.

The sketches have either been written in an allegorical style, as in the case of 'Castle Heart', or they are incidents taken from the Bible, put into a modern setting, and given little twists and turns to provoke thought and discussion. Christ before the Sanhedrin, for instance, has been set in the prohibition era of 1920s Chicago. He becomes Adam Fisher who is interrogated by three gangsters.

You'll find no jargon in the sketches, but a directness, mixed with a down-to-earth humour, which will appeal to a wide range of ages and intellects.

Each sketch has been written on the basis that simplicity of set layout is essential. Many of the sets should therefore take seconds to assemble, and one or two are positioned by the cast as an integral part of the performance.

The performance time for the sketches ranges between three and fifteen minutes.

Contents

1

The Set-up

This sketch explores the possibility of what may have happened had Christ been born in Chicago in the days of Prohibition.

Cast: CHARLEY GRECO
SAM SALINO
JOHNNY 'THE KNIFE' LORENZO
BARBERRA
ADAM FISHER

The scene is a room in downtown Chicago. A meeting of gangsters is taking place. Sitting at his desk is CHARLEY GRECO. *With him are* JOHNNY 'THE KNIFE' LORENZO, *and* SAM SALINO. CHARLEY *looks worried.*

CHARLEY   . . . So what you're saying, Sam, is that one of the things we gotta do for this amnesty is to hand over these guys to the Feds, right?

SAM   That's right, Boss, that's the word as I heard it.

CHARLEY   So then what happens?

JOHNNY   As I hear it, Boss, it's something to do with some State Anniversary. They wanna show the people of Chicago some good will, so they're gonna make a big thing about letting one of the guys go.

CHARLEY	So what happens to the other one?
JOHNNY	Aw, they throw him in the slammer or something.
CHARLEY	So where're these two guys now?
SAM	They're outside in the meat van. You want I should get 'em?
CHARLEY	You ought to transport them guys different. I'm getting complaints of contaminated pork 'cos of where you hang 'em in the van. *[General laughter.]*
SAM	*[Heading for the door]* Ya gotta be careful the way you hang these turkeys.
CHARLEY	Be careful you don't bruise the merchandise, Sam. *[SAM exits.]* ... Know anything about these two guys, Johnny?
JOHNNY	Seems like one of them, guy called Barberra, is a political aggravator ... that's what Sam called him.
CHARLEY	Where was you educated? The word is agitator, political agitator ... Never mind, I'll ask the guys themselves.
JOHNNY	Yeah, sorry Boss, I didn't know much more anyway. One of the guys ain't even said a word. *[He plays with a stiletto knife]* ... Not yet anyhow ...
CHARLEY	No dice, kid, these guys gotta be delivered to the Feds in A1 condition.
JOHNNY	*[Disappointed but putting the knife away]* Okay, Boss, just as you say. *[Re-enter SAM]*
SAM	I got them outside. Do you want them in one at a time?
CHARLEY	Yeah, let's see what these turkeys are stuffed with. *[SAM exits and brings in BARBERRA.]*

14

SAM   Stand there, kid.
              [He indicates a space in front of the desk.]
              The Boss wants to ask you one or two
              questions.
              [He stands behind BARBERRA.]

BARBERRA   Don't call me kid, I ain't no kid.

CHARLEY   Just button your mouth, kid, you ain't in no
              position to raise objections. We gotta decide
              what to do with you, see? If you know
              what's good for you, you'll do a bit of co-
              operating . . . Now, you gonna play ball with
              me, or do you want I should get Johnny here
              to stick you in the ice-maker till you cool
              down?

JOHNNY   *[feigning concern]* Are you sure you want me
              to do that, Boss? . . . I mean, last time I shut
              someone in there, the catch on the door bust,
              remember? The guy froze to death while we
              was trying to fix it.

CHARLEY   Well what d'ya say, kid, easy way or hard
              way?

BARBERRA   *[Sulkily]* Okay, what d'ya wanna know?
              *[CHARLEY walks round to the front of the desk
              and sits on the edge. JOHNNY stands and walks
              to behind the desk.]*

CHARLEY   That's better. So tell me what you've been
              doing to make the Feds think you been a
              naughty boy?

BARBERRA   Search me. I ain't done nothin'.

CHARLEY   *[Exasperated sigh]* Kid, d'you wanna answer
              me or d'you wanna spend eternity pickin'
              icicles off the end of your nose? WHAT DO
              THEY WANT YOU FOR?

BARBERRA   All I done was to talk politics with the kids.

CHARLEY   High school kids, right?
              [He stands and walks down right.]

15

BARBERRA   Yeah, any younger than that and the topic gets interrupted by diaper changes.

CHARLEY   *[ironic grin]* Hey, guys, we got some sort of joker here! *[abruptly serious]* You don't just talk to them though, do you? As I hear it, you show them how to make little ticking packages ... Sort of package that might be used to spread government vehicles all over the sidewalk when their little ringers go ding-a-ling.

BARBERRA   If you know so much, what you asking me for?

CHARLEY   So's I can hear your side of things, kid. So I can hear you put some sentences together. So ... I think it's highly commendable. *[sits on table]* Keeps the legal populace down in numbers. In fact, if I had a medal I'd be tempted to pin it on you ... but for one thing ... *[He sits and talks to the floor.]*
... That one thing is that some of these exploding clocks is liable one day to hurt some of my friends in the force.

[BARBERRA looks slightly surprised.]

... Oh yeah, kid, I got a few friends in high places ... Thing is, you could say that some of these friends have greatly assisted in business ventures of mine ... It might also interest you to know that only yesterday I was taking tea with our beloved Police Chief. He actually asked me if I could contact you with a view to asking you over to his place for tea. Seems like he's sent quite a few of his employees round to your place with a view to escorting you to his tea party, but you ain't ever been in. *[sits in his chair]*
... So I've been asked to send you round to

16

	see him in my car. You like riding in big limos? If you're very good, I might just let you ride up front, next to the driver.
SAM	You ought to say thank you to the Boss. You're lucky he ain't charging you the price of the gas for the trip.
CHARLEY	Okay, Sam, get him to wait outside while I talk to this other jerk.
SAM	Right you are, Boss.

[Turning BARBERRA round to face him]

You ever seen how people leave the room where there's a king? . . . No? . . . Oh! Well it's like this . . .

[Sam grasps BARBERRA and 'knees' him in the stomach, causing BARBERRA to double up. He then bows himself and still holding the doubled BARBERRA, exits backwards through the door.]

CHARLEY	That kid could come in useful to us you know, he's got spirit. Reminds me of me at that age . . . Still, the Feds want both and they're only gonna set one free. Let's see what the other guy's gotta say for himself.
JOHNNY	How do you think they decide which one to set free, Boss?
CHARLEY	I got an idea they get a body of upright citizens to decide which guy would most benefit society by being set loose.

[He searches for an example]

Like er . . . If they was to choose between you and me, they'd probably turn you loose 'cos er . . . *[he pulls a wry face and turns away from JOHNNY]* you got more talent than me!

JOHNNY	Gee, Boss, you really think so?

[CHARLEY looks heavenwards just as SAM enters with the second prisoner.]

SAM	Here he is . . . I don't know if you're gonna

get much out of him. He ain't said a word since we pulled him off the streets.

CHARLEY What's your name, kid? [*No reply.*]

Okay, Sam, d'ya wanna put some pressure on this kid for me, I'm running out of what little patience I woke up with this morning.

SAM It won't work with this one, Boss. We already tried a little persuasion on the way over here. He's either stupid or brave. I reckon on the first, 'cos i got most of the information I want from the guys on the street.

CHARLEY So you tell me what his name is, then.

SAM Goes by the name of Adam Fisher.

CHARLEY So why should the Feds want him?

SAM Seems like the guy's a bit of a vagrant. Never does no work for a living. Not legit anyhow . . . He's wanted for possible incitement to cause a riot, unlawful assembly, and drugs offences. They ain't quite sure if they can make the last one stick 'cos no one's caught the guy taking anything. He uh . . . he sees things other people don't . . . Rumour is he's eating funny mushrooms for breakfast, or something.

CHARLEY So what's his beef, political or religious? It's gotta be one or the other.

SAM Everyone who's had dealings with the guy reckons he's some sort of religious nut . . . Uh, I don't know whether it's really important to mention this, but he's got some sort of ambition to rule the world.

CHARLEY Yeah, yeah, yeah. That's told me what I wanna know. The guy's obviously screwy. That's no reason for the Feds to take an interest in him though, is it?

18

SAM	You wouldn't guess it to look at him, Boss, but he's got some sort of charisma that makes people want to follow him. He's got supporters all over Chicago. They seem to hang on his every word. Some of them ain't cranks either ... There is one thing you ain't gonna like though, Boss.
CHARLEY	Try me.
SAM	It's to do with the incitement to riot bit.
CHARLEY	What about it?
SAM	*[moving away from CHARLEY]* He was inciting to riot on your property.
CHARLEY	*[quietly]* Oh ... Tell me more.
SAM	You remember the incident about two weeks back, when your roulette and dice tables was turned over in the new building on 17th Avenue, the converted church building? ... Well ... *[he points to ADAM.]*
CHARLEY	*[standing slowly]* Oh ... So you're the guy who upset all those tables and my clients into the bargain? You're the little squealer who started the police raid that night?
	[He confronts ADAM face to face.]
	... Know something, kid? You caused one or two of my nearest and dearest to spend the night in beds which they wasn't accustomed to ... IN THE POLICE CELLS ...
	... Why did ya do it kid, huh? ... who gave you the authority to turn them roulette tables over?
ADAM	God.
	[There follows a long pause, during which CHARLEY stares blankly at ADAM.]
CHARLEY	You wanna try hitting me again with that? *[to SAM]* Did he say what I thought I heard

19

him say or did he swear? ... Take a look under his foot, Johnny, maybe he trod on a nail or something ...

[JOHNNY moves forward and lifts ADAM'S foot to look underneath. CHARLEY claps his hand to his head in disbelief as he obviously didn't intend JOHNNY to take him literally.]

JOHNNY   Nope, there ain't no nails or nothin' under his feet, Boss, but there's ...

CHARLEY   *[patiently to JOHNNY who is looking puzzled]* Okay, Johnny it's not important.
[to SAM] Get this kid outta here, before I do something I'll regret. Who does he think he is anyway?

ADAM   I am the son of man.

CHARLEY   Yeah and I'm a monkey's uncle ... Sam ... OUT ...

[SAM frog-marches ADAM towards the door.]

... Leave him with Joe outside and come back in here.

[SAM exits with ADAM and re-enters immediately alone.]

Sam, I want you to listen, and listen good. We can use this Barberra character. If the Feds got the kid to the grand jury, he'd go down for a long stretch. As I see it, that'd be an awful waste of talent ... Right, we got this amnesty, yeah? ... So, we done the Feds a favour, right? ... So I reckon they should do us a favour in return. Sam, do you know if they're getting some sort of a committee organised to decide which of the two to set loose after the Feds taken delivery from us?

SAM   As I heard it, Boss, they got invitations going out for the committee to meet day after tomorrow.

20

CHARLEY	*[resuming his seat]* Got any names to go on?
SAM	I can get the names by tonight, Boss.
CHARLEY	*[smiling]* Sam, I think we can put this little episode to good use. When you get names, I want you to pay a personal visit to each one of them. Get my drift? . . . But no rough stuff. Just show them your card and tell them it would be in their best interests to let Barberra go free.
SAM	Supposin' the Feds have already been to see them?
CHARLEY	Then you'll have to persuade them that what the Feds have to say is a load of baloney. Take Joe and Ricardo with you, they can be persuasive! . . . When they set Barberra free, bring him back here . . . Go to it, Sam.
	[SAM exits. There is a pause. CHARLEY notices JOHNNY'S puzzled expression.]
CHARLEY	What's up, kid? You look worried. Did I miss out on anything?
JOHNNY	Nothing like that, Boss, it's just that . . . Aw, it ain't nothin' I guess . . .
CHARLEY	Well, whatever it is, you'd better tell me.
JOHNNY	You know you told me to look see if there was any nails on the floor? . . . *[CHARLEY nods]* . . . Well I didn't find no nails . . .
CHARLEY	*[Exasperated]* No, kid, I think you missed the point, I never expected you to . . .
JOHNNY	. . . There was no nails, just the marks where nails had been . . .
CHARLEY	*[rising from his desk, and walking round to inspect the carpet]* Someone been sticking nails in my Persian rug, huh?
JOHNNY	*[to CHARLEY who is on his knees inspecting the carpet]* No, no, Boss, you got it all wrong. You see, the guy was wearing sandals.

That's why I saw the marks. There was no nail marks in the rug. The marks of the nails was in the guy's feet . . . both feet . . . all the way through . . .

[CHARLEY *stares at* JOHNNY.]

2

The Christmas Fairy?

This sketch is designed to help focus attention on the true meaning of Christmas and away from the commercialism which many of us may take for granted.

Cast: MAN
          CHARLADY (ANGEL)

The scene is set in a church. A CHARLADY appears in the church pulpit, and is seen to be cleaning it with a feather duster. She hums 'White Christmas' to herself. From one side of the church, a MAN enters. He is wearing a Christmas cracker hat and is looking around him in a puzzled way.
NB At the end of the sketch an alternative version is presented for acting in a church which has no pulpit but has a lectern.

MAN   Where on earth am I?
CHARLADY   Where do you think you are, love?
MAN   Well, obviously a church of some sort . . .
            But the last thing I remember was sitting
            down at home to watch the Queen's speech
            on television. I must have nodded off, I
            suppose.
CHARLADY   *[To herself]* Him and about 50 million other
            men around the world.
            [To him] The Queen's speech isn't the last
            thing you were watching before you drop-
            ped off though, is it?

23

MAN   Uh, no ... I was looking at the fairy on top of the Christmas tree.

CHARLADY Yes, and what were you thinking at the time?

MAN   I was wondering what she would have thought of it all if she could speak ... I mean, the Christmas fairy must see so many Christmasses in so many households throughout the world ... *[embarrassed]* Childish thought to have, I know.

CHARLADY Not at all ... as a matter of fact, it can get very nippy up there, I can tell you, especially if you happen to be billeted out to an Eskimo family at the North Pole.

MAN   Pardon?

CHARLADY Dear me, slow aren't we? If you look a bit closer you can see it was me you were looking at on top of that tree. This ... *[indicates the duster]* is only what I do the rest of the year.

MAN   What, cleaning?

         [Alternative version starting at this point can be found at the end of the sketch.]

CHARLADY Only pulpits dear, only pulpits. High pulpits at that. Going out of popularity nowadays though it seems. High ones, I mean. *[She looks around to see she's not overheard before continuing]* Between you and me, I reckon it's all these ageing clergymen. I don't think they relish the prospect of tackling all those stairs in their old age, you see ... Mind you, as I see it, if you're going to be looking down at earth from a great height in the near future anyway, you need to get in as much practice as you can ...

[Alternative version ends here and resume script.]

Anyway, you wanted to know what I thought of Christmas . . . When I'm up there on top of the Christmas tree, watching how some people celebrate Christmas, I wish at times that I was fixed so's to be pointing the other way.

MAN   But it's such a happy time . . . all those presents.

CHARLADY   No, no. It's not the presents, or the giving of them that make for a happy Christmas . . . I'll tell you something. There are many people whose Christmas would be complete if they could spend the day with someone they loved.

MAN   Yes, but what you've said applies to the elderly. Christmas is essentially for children, isn't it?

CHARLADY   There are children who spend Christmas separated from loved ones, as well you know . . .

MAN   Oh . . . *[Embarrassed]* . . . Yes, I'd forgotten those.

CHARLADY   A lot of people do forget them . . . I don't blame you for thinking that Christmas is for children, what with all the advertising . . . Christmas isn't just for children though . . . If you were to celebrate someone's birthday at your home, someone who wasn't able to attend for one reason or another, wouldn't you at some point drink a toast to that person's health?

MAN   But of course, it wouldn't be right not to.

CHARLADY   Okay, so whose birthday is it on Christmas day?

MAN   *[flustered]* It's . . . er . . . Christ's I suppose.

CHARLADY   I suppose, I suppose!! . . . Good heavens, man, the clue's there in the name, isn't it . . . Christ's mass? . . . *[shakes her head]* Dear me!

MAN   Sorry, I wasn't thinking . . . It must have been the heavy meal I just had.

CHARLADY   *[relenting]* All right, but don't you think it would be good to think about him for once this year?

MAN   *[after a pause]* Tell me something . . . If it's his birthday, why do we give each other presents?

CHARLADY   That's easy. It's a gesture. A sign that we care for the one we're giving the present to. A sign of how much we love that person. We're doing for someone else what Christ would do for all of us if he were here in person.

MAN   *[awed]* I never looked at it like that before!

CHARLADY   *[to herself]* That's because you never stopped to think.

MAN   Pardon?

CHARLADY   Nothing . . . *[she dusts a little more]* When I think of what I saw last Christmas . . . *[shakes her head]*

MAN   What about it?

CHARLADY   I was in one house . . . and the children! . . . The children were squabbling over each other's toys, and the parents were having a rare old go at each other over the equality of labour in the business of the food preparation! It was such a racket. They didn't have a good thought between them all day, let alone consider whose day it was!

MAN   Sounds a bit like our family ... *[he smiles]*
CHARLADY   *[matter of factly]* It *was* your family actually.
             [long pause]
             ... Expensive, wasn't it? ... Christmas?
MAN   I'll say. *[he walks over to the CHARLADY]*
             Good grief, when I think about it ...
             *[the CHARLADY stops dusting and looks expect-
             antly at the MAN]* ... Expensive's not the
             word for it ... Do you know, I reckon I've
             spent in the region of £500 this year. That's
             well up on last year.
CHARLADY   *[annoyed]* I wasn't thinking of you. I was
             thinking of the expense to Christ. If he
             hadn't died the way he did, you wouldn't be
             celebrating Christmas day ... *[she consults
             her watch]*
             ... Time's up, you've got to be getting back
             to your wife. Try not to forget our conversa-
             tion, will you?
               *[She gestures at the MAN who spins off the way
               he came in. She then smiles and looks heaven-
               wards and puts down her duster.]*
             He thought he was talking to a fairy. *[She
             laughs]*
             ... Isn't it funny how people mistake your
             birth star for a magic wand! ... Nothing to
             do with magic at all, is it?
             *[She picks up a stick with a glittering star on the
             top. It appears as though the feather duster has
             been transformed.]*
             ... Well, I must fly. I've got another pulpit
             to clean, and another Dad to meet before I
             get back ... Mmm, angel cake for tea to-
             night ... *[she exits]*.

CHARLADY   Only lecterns, only lecterns. It's an acquired skill you know to clean some of these things. All the crooks and nannies. ... I mean nooks and crannies. When I'm faced with some of these things, I know it's about time to bring my secret weapon into action.

MAN   And what might that be?

CHARLADY   My secret weapon?

MAN   *[nodding]* Mmm.

CHARLADY   It's an old toothbrush dipped in cleaning fluid. You keep that to yourself though ... trade secret.

3

The Extraordinary Meeting

Pentecost to the Jewish authorities must have posed a very awkward problem. How were they to deal with such an unprecedented occurrence? This sketch is a modern interpretation of the sorts of questions which may have been asked. The Jewish leaders are replaced by factory management, and the first converts are substituted by a factory workforce. The original sketch was written with a view to giving the factory workforce northern accents, and the management spoke with parodied 'upper class' accents.

Cast:
    PETER
    LAZARUS
    JOHN
    ANNAS
    CAIAPHAS
    DESPATCH RIDER
    OTHER DISCIPLES

The scene is a union meeting. A number of workers are gathered listening to the union shop floor representative [PETER].

SCENE ONE

PETER   I think you all know why we're gathered here today, brothers. We're all aware that the man we came to admire over the past three years has been ousted from his position alongside us in our place of work ... Now, I've called this meeting to say that, shortly before going to join his Father at Head Office, our friend Jesus left us a message which I've been asked to read out to you ... Before I start, I would remind you that this meeting has been convened in secret ... Management have not been informed for obvious reasons ...

LAZARUS   [standing angrily] Quite right too, brothers, it was Management that got rid of Jesus, them and their bully-boy tactics.

JOHN   All right, Lazarus, we know you owe a lot to Jesus, but let's discuss this rationally.

LAZARUS   If Management had known who they were trying to get rid of, John, they'd have thought twice, I can tell you.

JOHN   They were told, Lazarus. All they wanted him to do was to prove his identity. They wouldn't take his word for it.

LAZARUS   We took his word for it, didn't we? ...

PETER   [interrupting] ... Come on, lads, let's have a bit of order, shall we? You're forgetting one thing, both of you ... Jesus joined our organisation to see what conditions we were working under, and see them in a true light. If he'd made it known that he was the owner's son as soon as he got here, he

wouldn't have seen the true conditions we work under.

LAZARUS   Yes, but they must have known at some point who he was. Look what he did for us.

PETER   I can't answer for what went through Management's mind, I'm afraid . . . I do think we're digressing a bit though. Let's get on, shall we? . . .

[murmurs of assent]

. . . *[reading]* Fellow workers, by the time you read this I'll be sitting in my Father's office, discussing my time with you. I've had the pleasure of working with you for the past three years and I'm not about to forget you in the years to come. Though I can't be with you in person, I intend to be with you in spirit. I'm asking you, through Peter, to organise a sit-in at Mary's house for the next few days until you hear from me. Yours faithfully, Jesus.

[PETER puts the letter into his pocket.]

. . . Right, Ladies and Gentlemen, I've asked Mary, and she's kindly consented to loan us her upper room for however long it takes. Now, can I have a show of hands for numbers staying; we'll need it for catering purposes.

[All hands go up.]

. . . Unanimous, that makes things easier . . . Right, if you'd all like to follow me, we'll adjourn to the upstairs room.

[Inside the Management Office, some days later. Two men are seated at a table looking bored. One is playing with a pencil.]

ANNAS   Very quiet, isn't it, Caiaphas old chap?

CAIAPHAS   I'll say, now that the militant faction aren't turning up for work.

ANNAS   Any chance of them coming back in the near future?

CAIAPHAS   The question is, do we really want them back? Funny how they seem to have just disappeared off the face of the earth, though.

ANNAS   Don't suppose anyone's heard anything of Barabbas?

CAIAPHAS   Rumour has it that he was last seen hijacking camels in the Kalahari Desert, and holding them for ransom.

ANNAS   *[After a thoughtful pause]* Jolly quiet though, isn't it? I get a funny feeling that something is brewing somewhere.
    [There is a knock at the door.] Come in . . .
    [A despatch rider enters wearing a crash helmet.]

DESPATCH RIDER   Got a camelgram 'ere for a Mr Caiaphas, Priest.

CAIAPHAS   That'll be for me.

RIDER   You got proof of your identity then, 'ave you?

CAIAPHAS   *[pulling down the back of his shirt collar]* What does that say?

RIDER   'Marcus and Spencerus.'

CAIAPHAS   No, no, underneath.

RIDER   Oh yeah, right. 'Ere you are then.
    [He hands the letter over and exits.]

CAIAPHAS	*[reading]* Oh no!
ANNAS	What's the matter, old man?
CAIAPHAS	They're out, that's what's the matter. Out on the streets, in force . . .
ANNAS	What are you blithering on about, old man? Who's out?
CAIAPHAS	The militant tendency, the strikers. According to this *[indicates letter]* they've erupted onto the streets in large numbers. And what's more, they've learnt to speak in foreign languages, goodness knows how or where.
ANNAS	*[shocked]* Good grief, that means they'll be calling us names and we won't know what they're saying!
CAIAPHAS	The implications are far worse than that, I'm afraid. According to this, they're out telling everyone that we've refused to recognise that the owner's son was working here for three years, and that we've conspired to get rid of him behind the backs of the workforce.
ANNAS	*[More shocked]* What? . . . Bu . . . Bu . . . Er . . . Er . . .
CAIAPHAS	Exactly, and if you think that's bad news, you wait till you hear that their leader is with them in spirit but not in person.
ANNAS	Oh that's silly. How are we supposed to deal with a leader we can't see? It's no good, we'll just have to send the security guards out to give our little breakaway group a persuasive talking to *[he smiles cynically]* . . . if you get my drift . . . How long have they been out on the streets?

CAIAPHAS	Since nine this morning. Half a day now ... But according to this, the answer's not that easy.
ANNAS	Why not? What's stopping us?
CAIAPHAS	How many guards have we available?
ANNAS	About twenty. More than enough to deal with a hundred and twenty break-away members, surely?
CAIAPHAS	*[laughing]* I wish that there were only a hundred odd people to deal with. *[handing him the letter]* You'd better read it for yourself.
ANNAS	*[reads aloud]* ... Having assessed the ... *[mutter, mutter]* ... and seeing fit in the circumstances ... *[mutter, mutter]* ... We have to report that in the space of this morning's events, the small band of dissident Israelites have won over to their cause a following numbering in excess of ... *[Annas slumps into a seat as he says the following]* ... Three thousand men, women and children ... !
CAIAPHAS	Do you still think I should order out the security guards?
ANNAS	*[after a long pause]* Maybe if we ignore it, the problem might go away ...

4

Is the Price Right?

This sketch represents, quite simply, the trial of Christ carried out in the form of a quiz programme.

Many of the televised quiz shows we see are very largely rehearsed affairs, with audiences being given cues when to laugh, when to applaud, etc.

This, to put it mildly, is a form of studio audience manipulation, carried out by the various show producers to help relay an atmosphere to the home audience.

What the television viewer doesn't see is the work carried out with the studio audience, both before and during the recording of the programme.

With this form of manipulation in mind, and remembering how 'a number of priests stirred up the crowd and shouted for the crucifixion of Christ', the comparison between the trial and the quiz programme becomes evident.

In the sketch we have symbolic characters, for example Herod becomes the Floor Producer; the 'Audience Prompt' is called Eve (the reason why becomes apparent) and the six latecomers take the place of the priests who 'stirred up the crowd'.

NB The sketch should be played at a fast and furious pace, giving the audience no time to think of clues to the outcome.

Cast: PRODUCER (H E RODSWAY)
               EVE
               CAMERAMAN
               MONTY PILATE
               6 AUDIENCE 'PLANTS'
               BARABBAS
               JESUS
               GUARD

The scene is a quiz studio. On set, and placed in a central position, are two boxes with question marks printed on the sides facing the audience. A camera and tripod are placed to one side, facing the set.

At the beginning of the sketch EVE, the Audience Prompt, enters and walks to the opposite side of the set to the camera carrying her 'prompting boards'. Following her we have the floor PRODUCER, who in turn is followed by the CAMERAMAN. Both the PRODUCER and the CAMERAMAN are wearing 'headphones' draped around their necks. The PRODUCER engages in a short discussion with EVE before turning his attention to the audience.

PRODUCER   Good evening, ladies and gentlemen. May
               I take this opportunity of welcoming you,
               the studio audience, to this edition of the
               quiz programme, 'Is the Price Right?'
                   I'll just start by making the introductions
               so you know who's who ... I'm Henry
               Rodsway, otherwise known as Rod to the
               rest of the resident staff here, and I'm
               what is known as the Floor Producer of
               the programme. It's my job to keep things
               chugging along and in a moment I'll be
               giving you a briefing as to certain proce-
               dures we want you all to follow ... Over
               there we have Eve Willsden, the Audience
               Prompt; and on camera we have John

Alexander. As you all know, this is a live programme, relayed from here Tele Jerusalem in ... *[consults watch]* Ooh ... roughly five minutes from now, so I haven't too long to explain things. Right, the Audience Prompt, during the run of the programme will, from time to time, hold up instructions on boards which we ask you to comply with ... Show them a typical one, Eve.

[EVE holds up a board which reads 'APPLAUSE'.]

Quite simply, we'd like you to applaud when such a board is raised. We try not to be too dictatorial on these programmes, you'll get into the swing of it as we proceed. One thing I would ask you, though, and that is to obey the instruction immediately on seeing it, and to stop when Eve lowers the board.

[consults watch]

... As we don't have much time left, I'll pass you over to John on the camera for his briefing.

[He is about to hand over, but remembers something.]

... Oh, and by the way, don't take any notice of me during the show, I'll be running back and forth waving instructions to the crew ... John.

[As the PRODUCER walks away, he adjusts the headphones to cover his ears. His actions then convey that he is talking to a central studio elsewhere throughout the CAMERAMAN's briefing.]

CAMERAMAN   *[Walking to centre]* Very simple instructions

on my part, ladies and gentlemen. *[points to camera]* Occasionally, during the show, I'll be panning or turning the camera on to you the audience to show the viewers at home how much you're enjoying the show. Just keep smiling please, and try to avoid looking at the camera or mouthing the words 'Hello Mum'. It makes a mockery of the show. Okay, that's all I have to say. I'll hand you back to Rod.

[He waves PRODUCER forward. As he comes down set he slides the headphones back on to his shoulders.]

PRODUCER We still have a couple of minutes left to us, so, Eve, throw up a couple of boards, would you? See how they do.

[There follows a few improvised moments during which the audience practise their applause or laughter.]

Right, I think we're ready to go . . .

[At this point the PRODUCER discreetly indicates to the back of the hall or room. As he turns away and occupies himself with 'business', about six or more people enter the auditorium and swiftly disperse themselves among the other seated onlookers. Their task becomes apparent later. When they are settled, the PRODUCER turns back to face the audience seemingly unaware of the new faces.]

. . . We'll be under way in thirty seconds everyone.

[EVE and the CAMERAMAN become businesslike.]

. . . Get ready to watch for the boards everyone, and prepare yourself to give

38

your host 'MONTY PILATE' the biggest rip-
roaring welcome you can muster.

[He dons his headphones.]

... Okay Studio *[looks at watch]*

... Cue music ... Cue titles ... Roll
'em ...

*[He runs to the back of the set where MONTY
is to make his entrance and says]* Okay
Monty, ready when you are ...

[He turns to the audience] Ladies and
gentlemen, your host, Monty Pilate ...

*[He indicates to EVE who holds up a board
reading, 'APPLAUSE'. MONTY PILATE immediately makes a flamboyant entrance.
The 'latecomers' now reveal their purpose.
They stand at any sign of a prompt board
and display excessive exuberance, at the
same time inciting the crowd in their
immediate vicinity to join in ... MONTY
runs down to the front, holding his hands
up in a mock silencing gesture.]*

MONTY Welcome, welcome everybody ... Oh too
much, too much. Thank you, thank you
for such a warm welcome ...

*[The applause board is lowered at a gesture
from the PRODUCER. MONTY now speaks next
to camera.]*

... And welcome all you at home to another edition of 'Is the Price Right?' ...
Tonight is a very special night, because it's
being sponsored by none other than our
Prison Authorities!

*[The PRODUCER indicates to EVE, who holds
up a board reading 'Ooooooh'. The audience
comply.]*

... A special mention is given here to our

39

High Priest, Caiaphas for nominating tonight's contestants.

[to camera] Sorry you couldn't be with us
tonight, Caiaphas ... Hope the migraine
clears up soon, old son! ...

[to live audience]

... So, as a first on Tele Jerusalem, or for
that matter, a first on any quiz, let's have a
big hand for tonight's contestants ... Two
criminals!

*[EVE is indicated by the PRODUCER and she
lifts an 'APPLAUSE' board as MONTY says]*

... Come on down ...

*[JESUS and BARABBAS enter and go to either
side of MONTY. When in place, the board is
lowered.]*

... On my left, we have Barabbas, and on
my right, Jesus of Nazareth ...

*[Short applause as MONTY walks forward to
the two boxes.]*

... As we go straight into the game, a
quick reminder of the rules. Inside each of
these boxes is an envelope, inside of
which, in turn, is a key. That key could be
the answer to a dream come true or a key
to failure ... For our studio audience and
for you at home, this is what is inside this
[indicates] box, and please don't shout
out, audience.

*[He indicates the box to his right, as EVE
holds up a card to the camera and then to the
audience which reads, 'The key to freedom'.
The latecomers let out cries of 'Oooooh'.]*

... and in the other box we have ...

*[EVE swops the board for one which reads,
'The key to eternity', and goes through the*

40

same routine as previously to general cries of
'Ooooh'.]

... Now, as you know, studio audience,
you are free to interpret the prize how you
will. It's up to you what the prize will take
the form of ...

... All right, gentlemen, you know the
rules ... I have three questions here, and
you have three seconds in which to answer
each question. If at the end of those three
seconds the question remains unanswered,
you'll hear this sound ...

[EVE bangs a gong.]

... If I hear that sound, I'm afraid you
forfeit the mark. The person who answers
the most questions wins the box of his
choice. Do you understand, gentlemen?

[BARABBAS nods, JESUS does not respond.]

... All righty, the first question goes to
you Barabbas. Are you ready?

BARABBAS	Uh huh.
MONTY	Pay attention now ...

[MONTY slows his speech so there is no
question of misinterpretation.]

... Is it true ... that you have been con-
victed ... in the past ... of robbery?

BARABBAS	[Smiling, matter of factly] That is true, cer-
tainly.
MONTY	[to audience in amazement] Word for word,
what I have on this card!

[The PRODUCER immediately indicates to
EVE who holds up 'APPLAUSE'. The 'latecomers' cheer loudly. At this point, the
camera is turned on to the audience. As
the camera pans, each 'latecomer' hides his
face to avoid identity. The prompt board is

lowered as the camera returns to point at MONTY.]

... Jesus of Nazareth, your first question is this ... Have you ever caused a disturbance ... or incited a riot ... within the confines of the Temple?

[*The* PRODUCER *is seen to count the seconds on his watch while* MONTY *looks to* JESUS *expectantly. At the end of four seconds* EVE *sounds the gong. The* PRODUCER *then indicates for the next board, which* EVE *lifts. It reads 'BOO, HISS'. As the 'crowd' correspond,* MONTY *looks at them with a puzzled expression, but soon returns to the questioning.*]

... Okay, Barabbas, second question ... Do you belong to a terrorist organisation ... intent on home rule for the Jews?

BARABBAS [*confidently*] But of course.

[EVE *now holds up* 'APPLAUSE'. *The camera pans and the same sequence of events is repeated as for* BARABBAS' *first question.*]

MONTY Your second question, Jesus of Nazareth, is this ... Have you ever ... committed miracles ... or done any other work ... such as healing the sick ... on the Sabbath?

[*There is no reply, and when the gong is sounded for the second time the 'latecomers' start to boo and hiss with no prompt from* EVE. MONTY *hurries on.*]

... Err Barabbas, your third question is this ... Have you ever murdered, I repeat, murdered ... to further the aims of your terrorist organisation?

BARABBAS [*brazenly*] Why, yes.

[*The* 'APPLAUSE' *goes up.* MONTY *looks at*

	BARABBAS with a look of doubt and looks with suspicion at the PRODUCER. He turns to JESUS when the applause dies.]
MONTY	Your third and final question, Jesus of Nazareth, is ... Do you think you are ... or have ever professed to be ... the King of the Jews? ...
	[After four seconds the gong sounds and there is a silence, with no instructions from EVE.]
	... The end of the contest, ladies and gentlemen, and the score looks like this ... Three to Barabbas, and nil to Jesus of Nazareth ...
	[The 'APPLAUSE' board is lifted.]
	... Okay, Barabbas, which box do you want me to open for you? Which box should he open, everybody?
	[The PRODUCER indicates for the audience to choose the box on the left. The 'latecomers' start to chant, 'The one on the left.' The PRODUCER holds up his hand for the chant to stop after an appropriate interval.]
BARABBAS	I'll have this one.
MONTY	*[reaching into the box and selecting an envelope]* You have won ... The key to freedom ...
	[Loud cheers from the audience.]
	... Let's leave it to the audience to tell us and the folks at home what they would like for our friend Barabbas. Okay, what do you want?
	[The camera turns round to the audience as the PRODUCER indicates to EVE. She lifts a board which states, 'SET HIM FREE.' A chant is set up and the phrase is repeated two or three times.]

. . . Okay you've told us what you want for Barabbas, now how about a little of the same for Jesus of Nazareth, as I tell you that his key is . . .

[*Opening the envelope.*]

. . . 'The key to eternity' . . .

[*A board is now held up which reads, 'CRUCIFY HIM'. The 'latecomers' lead a very loud chanting of the phrase until the* PRODUCER *indicates for the board to be lowered. During the chanting, the camera pans over the audience, with the 'latecomers' trying to avoid being recognised.* MONTY *looks staggered at this outcry but keeps calm.*]

. . . Well, there you are, ladies and gentlemen, the studio audience have given their verdict and who am I to argue with that? . . . It's Monty Pilate from 'Is the Price Right?' saying, good night and keep smiling . . .

[BARABBAS *leaves the set and walks down the aisle or auditorium, a free man. He is greeted with rapturous cheering from the 'latecomers' who crowd round him and accompany him out.* JESUS, *however, is led out in the opposite direction by a guard who appears at his side.* MONTY *throws down his script and runs over to remonstrate with the* PRODUCER. *The* PRODUCER *puts an arm around* MONTY's *shoulder and leads him off, trying to calm him. The* CAMERAMAN *and* EVE *pick up their equipment and exit.*]

5

Green Light for Go

This sketch is designed to show the work of Christ in our lives, and how we sometimes tend to operate on our own instincts rather than trusting in God's prompting.

In the sketch we see that the pilot of the aircraft is represented by the 'pilot of the Spirit of Trust' (Holy Spirit). Base headquarters represents God, and the passengers are indicative of God's people prior to mission.

Cast: PILOT
                SERGEANT
                JOHN
                WOMAN
                MIKE
                THOMAS
                PASSENGERS

The scene is the inside of a Hercules Transporter aircraft. To one side, the PILOT *sits sideways to the audience. He is holding an imaginary control stick. Behind is a screen dividing him from the main body of the aircraft where* PASSENGERS *wearing rucksacks (parachutes) are seated in a line facing the audience. The imaginary exit door of the plane is at the opposite end to the* PILOT, *and seated nearest to the door is the* SERGEANT. *His task is to see the* PASSENGERS *safely through the exit door when the green light flashes on.* NOTE: *To achieve the sound of an aircraft engine, a simple recording of a vacuum cleaner can be played as background noise.*

PILOT   *[Speaking into an imaginary intercom]* This is the pilot of the Spirit of Trust speaking. I'm your pilot for this trip. You should know that all your training is about to be put to the test. This is not a practice run. I repeat, not a practice run. You will shortly be dropped behind enemy lines. Prepare yourselves for action. We'll be reaching the drop zone in approximately two minutes . . . Get ready back there . . . See you in heaven when it's all over.

JOHN   *[standing, concerned]* I say, what is all this? I expected it to be a simple practice jump for charity. Nobody said anything about being dropped into the middle of a war!

WOMAN   None of us quite knows what to expect when we set out on these missions.

JOHN   But a battle is something entirely different from a drop for charity.

SERGEANT Right, make sure your harnesses are secure. I don't want to have to stop halfway down to give anyone a piggyback ride.
         [The SERGEANT stands with the others. They check their equipment and, on completion of inspection, they all hook imaginary rip cords to a bar above them and turn to face the drop/exit doors.]

MIKE   Sarge?

SERGEANT Yep, what's up, Mike?

MIKE   How do we know where we're jumping? It's pitch black out there. Most of us have never done a night drop before. We don't know what we're letting ourselves in for, do we?

SERGEANT Don't you worry about things like that. We've got a good pilot there. His job's to look out for

46

	ground flares and when he sees them, he gives us the green light. That's when we jump.
PILOT	*[over the intercom]* Okay, we're over the drop zone now. I can't see any flares yet but I'll keep you posted.
JOHN	How can we be over the drop zone if there are no flares showing?
SERGEANT	Don't worry about things like that, John, we've got an excellent man up front. He's been this way before, should know what he's doing. *[Pause.]*
PILOT	*[over the intercom]* Stand by.
JOHN	We are standing by, aren't we?
SERGEANT	Don't get in a flap. I don't like the delay either, you know. *[The SERGEANT turns away, obviously agitated by the wait.]*
PILOT	Still no sign of the flare yet.
THOMAS	*[the last person in the line]* Are you sure he knows what he's doing, Sarge? We seem to have been waiting an awful long time.
SERGEANT	It's all right, Thomas, I'm sure we'll get the green light in a minute. *[The SERGEANT becomes more agitated.]*
PILOT	Looks like flares ahead. Get ready back there . . . *[Everyone huddles together in preparation for the jump.]* . . . as you were, reflection of the moon off a lake.
JOHN	What is this? Some sort of test or something? It's no good for the nerves, I know that! *[The SERGEANT, now under stress, leans forward to look out of the drop doors.]*
THOMAS	Can you see anything, Sarge? Is there a lake down there? I didn't know we were going to be going over any lakes on the way!

SERGEANT	Neither did I, Thomas, neither did I. I can't see a thing down there myself. We must be getting the green light soon, surely!
PILOT	*[after another pause]* Flare ahead . . . Red light on, and starting count down to green light . . .
	[The people look up to an imaginary green light, and shuffle towards the door, ready to jump.]
	. . . Okay, 5 . . . 4 . . . 3 . . . 2 . . . 1 . . . Green light on, go, go, go.
	[The SERGEANT immediately steps back from the edge, pushing everyone back behind him as he does so. He holds up a restraining hand.]
SERGEANT	No go, I'm calling it off, return to your seats . . .
	[Everyone returns to their seats looking puzzled and unclipping their imaginary rip cords as they sit. The SERGEANT picks up the intercom to the PILOT and speaks. This makes the PILOT sit up, as he is not expecting anyone to be still on the aircraft.]
SERGEANT	Sergeant Smith here. I've stopped the jump.
PILOT	*[angry]* What do you mean, you've stopped the jump? I gave you the green light, you should be on your way.
SERGEANT	Couldn't see the flare . . . And we were waiting too long. Are you sure it was a flare you saw?
PILOT	You go on my say so, not on your judgement. I saw the flare, and that's a positive indication for you to go . . .
SERGEANT	Are you sure it wasn't another reflection? I couldn't see any sign of a light from a flare.
PILOT	*[calmly and slowly]* It just so happens that you wouldn't have seen the flare from where you are. You should have gone on the order. Your task is to carry out instructions on trust . . .

[*Pause, while the importance of this statement sinks in to the* SERGEANT.]

... All right, it's too late now. We're on our way home, not enough fuel for a second run. We'll have to try again another day.

[*The* SERGEANT *slowly puts his intercom down and sits in his place as the others watch him in silence. The* PILOT *leans across to speak into a secondary radio.*]

PILOT   Spirit to God, Spirit to God ... Abandoned drop. I repeat, abandoned drop. Mission abandoned due to non-compliance with pilot instructions ... I repeat ... Mission abandoned due to non-compliance with pilot instructions ... Over and out ...

[*He replaces the radio mike and picks up the intercom again.*]

... Sergeant? ...

[*The* SERGEANT *slowly walks over to the intercom with the rest watching him.*]

SERGEANT   [*speaking into the intercom*] Speaking ...

PILOT   I think you'd do well to remember that this operation has been a long time in the planning. I just hope that your lack of faith, and individual action, doesn't prolong the battle, that's all ...

[*The* PILOT *puts down the intercom and the* SERGEANT *turns back to the people.*]

SERGEANT   [*in angry frustration*] Don't look at me like that! It's not my fault. I reckon we'd have been in trouble if we'd gone ...

[*as he sits*] You know what they say, 'If in doubt, don't.'

JOHN   It doesn't bother me. I wouldn't have come if I'd known it was to be a real battle. It's not my war, after all.

49

WOMAN   What about the people down there who were expecting us though? I suppose it doesn't do to think of them?

[*The* SERGEANT *and* JOHN *turn away in embarrassment.*]

6

Calvary Hill School

The day of Pentecost ... We have no real accounts of the personal sensations experienced by witnesses of that day. We can however guess at its devastating effect from the statement in Acts, 'Those who accepted the message of the gospel that day were 3,000 in number.'

This sketch explores in an up-to-date manner a situation which might have occurred in a school classroom in Jerusalem, shortly after the death of Christ. The classroom in question is largely based on one which you might expect to find in the television series *Grange Hill*, and so the characters of the children should be well defined.

Cast: ANNOUNCER (a pupil)
                    TEACHER
                    RUTH
                    JOSHUA JUNIOR
                    SIMEON
                    4 PUPILS
                    MATTHEW
                    LUKE
                    MARTHA

At the beginning of the sketch, the children enter making a typical classroom din. They bring their own chairs which are set in file pattern facing the audience.

NB *At first sight this setting would call for the* TEACHER *to play with her back to the audience. To counter this, it's advisable for her to move up and down the aisles between the pupils during the sketch. After they've taken their places one child stands and walks to the front of the class to make an announcement to the audience. As the noise from the classroom persists, the child in question turns and shouts 'Oi!' The class instantly freezes.*

ANNOUNCER   *[turning to the audience and announcing officially]* A classroom in Jerusalem two months after the death of Christ.
             [an aside, not so officially] . . . 'Ere, you'll 'ave to forgive the modern outfits, only the costume hirers were fresh out of two-thousand-year-old school uniforms.
             [Turning back to the class, the ANNOUNCER *resumes his or her seat, saying 'Okay'. The noise and action resume. As the hubbub continues, one of the pupils starts to throw paper planes around the room.* TEACHER *enters just as one of the planes flies past her nose. The classroom goes quiet and she makes her way to one side of the set where there is a positioned table. She places one or two books on the table and turns back to the class.]*

TEACHER   RIGHT . . . Which one of you threw that papyrus plane?

RUTH   Please, Miss, no one, Miss . . .

TEACHER   If I've told you once, I've told you a thousand times to stand up when you talk to me, Ruth. I like to know who it is speaking. Now, stand up and repeat.

RUTH   *[standing]* Please, Miss, I said no one threw it, Miss.
             [She sits.]

52

TEACHER	What do you mean, no one threw it? Someone must have thrown it.
JOSHUA JUNIOR	[standing] She's right, Miss, no one threw it.
TEACHER	Are you trying to tell me that I'm seeing things, Joshua Junior?
JOSHUA JUNIOR	That's right, Miss. It's a figment of your imagination. It's bound to be because it'll be another 2,000 years before the aeroplane is invented.
	[He turns to the class, grins, and sits down.]
TEACHER	Oh ... Oh dear ... Well, in that case I'd better postpone today's lesson in aerodynamics ...
PUPIL 1	Whatever that is ...
TEACHER	Yes, exactly ...
	[She walks to her desk and looks through some notes before turning back.]
	... Very well, take out your exercise tablets, we'll refresh ourselves on the Law.
	[All the pupils groan, but produce bits of stone from convenient places.]
PUPIL 1	Quick someone, invent the aeroplane.
TEACHER	It's no good complaining, you can blame Joshua Junior for setting back the progress of mankind by 2,000 years. Now ... [she points to a pupil] ... Simeon, we'll start at the beginning, if you please.
SIMEON	[standing and reading] You shall have no other God but me.
	[Sits, as TEACHER picks out another pupil.]
PUPIL 1	[standing] You shall not create idols and worship them.
	[TEACHER points to another child.]

PUPIL 2	*[standing]* You shall not take the name of God in vain.
	[sits]
PUPIL 3	You must keep the Sabbath day holy.
JOSHUA JUNIOR	*[standing slowly]* Honour your parents.
	[He is about to sit when a voice comes from directly behind him.]
PUPIL 1	'Bout time you started then, innit Josh?
	[JOSHUA turns round and grabs hold of the pupil's lapels. At the same time the TEACHER bends down to pick something off the floor which she has noticed. While JOSHUA is threatening the pupil, another stands and quickly reads off the next commandment.]
PUPIL 4	. . . You shall not commit murder.
	[JOSHUA puts the pupil down.]
TEACHER	*[standing with a tablet in her hand, angrily]* Who has written this?
	[Silence from the class.]
	. . . Who has been writing on a school tablet the words, 'Jesus Christ is alive'? . . . Someone had better own up to this, or all of you will suffer for it as a group . . . You'll all be kept in after school, I warn you.
	[A pupil stands at the back.]
MATTHEW	It was me, Miss.
TEACHER	So, it was you, was it, Matthew? I might have guessed. Why? What is the meaning of this?
MATTHEW	Just thought I'd let everyone know, Miss, that's all.
TEACHER	Know what?
MATTHEW	What's written on there, Miss.
TEACHER	*[slowly, as if talking to an imbecile]* What is written on there is a lie, you stupid boy.

	Jesus of Nazareth was crucified two months ago, and nobody can live through that.
MATTHEW	*[calmly]* He didn't, Miss, that's just it, he didn't live through it.
TEACHER	*[looking skywards]* The boy's talking in riddles. It may interest you to know, boy, that my uncle, who just happens to be the High Priest Caiaphas, believes that this nation should be grateful we're rid of such a troublemaker. Now he's dead and gone, we should be rejoicing.
MATTHEW	*[eagerly]* Oh we are, Miss. My dad and his friends have been rejoicing all over the place for a couple of weeks now.
TEACHER	So I should think . . .
MATTHEW	. . . Yeah but not because Jesus is dead . . .
TEACHER	What? . . . Make sense, boy.
	[Another pupil stands.]
LUKE	What he's trying to say, Miss, is that his dad and my dad, and lots of our mums and dads have seen Jesus living after he was dead. He's proved to us all that death isn't the end of everything, it's just the beginning of the next life.
TEACHER	Oh don't be so stupid, Luke. Where is the man then if he's supposed to be alive?
LUKE	He's not here any more, Miss, not so's you can see him anyhow. His earthly body's gone to be with God.
TEACHER	*[temper]* Right, I've heard enough. I'll teach you that you can't afford to make a fool out of me. What rubbish! To expect me to fall for an idiotic story like that. What do you take me for? To assume I'd fall for a story about a dead man coming

back to life ... Gone to be with God indeed ... Prove to me a dead man can come back to life, and I'll show you a pink elephant.

[MARTHA stands bravely.]

... What's the matter with you?

MARTHA   I can, Miss.

TEACHER   You can what?

MARTHA   I can prove that a dead man can come back to life, Miss.

TEACHER   This is a conspiracy ... You're the new girl, aren't you? ... If you're going to tell me that Jesus has decided that he's going to make a quick trip from heaven to earth to prove a point ...

MARTHA   *[interrupting]* ... No, Miss, not Jesus ... My dad. It's my dad that died, but he's better now, thank you.

TEACHER   That's it ... that is it ... You're all trying to make a fool of me. Right, from now until the end of school, you'll all sit in silence with your hands on your heads.

              [MARTHA sits, and everyone slowly complies in putting their hands on their heads. TEACHER resumes her seat at the front of class and starts marking a pile of work. She looks up after a while.]

              ... You girl ... Yes you, the new girl. Stand up again ... Keep your hands on your head ... Now ...

              [She leans down with her pen to the register.]

              ... What's your name for the register?

MARTHA   Martha, Miss.

TEACHER   Mar ... tha ... And your father's name?

MARTHA   His name's Lazarus, Miss.

56

[*The* TEACHER *looks up slowly as it dawns on her. A voice comes from the back of the class.*]

VOICE   [*with heavy sarcasm*] 'Ere, Miss. When Martha's dad comes to pick her up at the end of school today, will you be showing us that pink elephant you were telling us about?

[*Everyone cheers as* TEACHER *picks up her books and walks swiftly out with a harassed expression. The children pick up their chairs and follow, making a general din.*]

7

The Shepherds' Nativity

This sketch rather speaks for itself. To be performed at Christmas, it involves shepherds who, strangely enough, possess West Country dialects!

Cast:

NATHAN
WALTER
DAN
ANGEL
THREE OTHER SHEPHERDS
MARY
JOSEPH
BABY JESUS

[*Enter three shepherds from the side, dressed in smocks.*]

NATHAN   [*to following shepherd on surveying the audience*] Looks like these is the ones, Walter.

WALTER   Ah, you be right there, Nathan.

DAN   [*Squinting*] Funny looking bunch if you asks I!

NATHAN   Now don't you go being rude, our Dan. These good people are modern, that's all ... They ain't like you and I.
          [*He moves forward to address the audience.*]

	... We bin sent to tell you about our bit of good fortune, ain't we lads?
WALTER AND DAN	Ar ... Ar ...
NATHAN	*[Proudly]* We've come to tell you that we three 'ad the good fortune a couple of thousand years ago, of meeting the baby infant who was to grow up to be the Messiah, didn't we, lads?
WALTER AND DAN	*[Swollen with pride]* Ar ... Ar ...
	[Long pause while the three shepherds wait for an audience reaction.]
WALTER	*[eventually]* What did I tell you, Nathan? I knew they wouldn't know what you was on about. It doesn't mean a thing to them.
DAN	I don't reckon you'd better say nothing else, our Nat. If you were to start telling them about the angels and all that singing around the camp fire, we're bound to land up in the sheep dip again.
WALTER	'Ere I don't want to end up there! Come on, let's leave while the going's good.
DAN	Yeah, I'm for that all right ... Which way should we head, Nat, west?
WALTER	*[misunderstanding]* Don't be daft, our Dan! He's got an overdraft in the Nat West. I reckon we ought to go this way ...
NATHAN	... Will you two be quiet a minute *[the two go quiet]* ... Right, I should think so ... We're gonna have to put plan B into operation.
DAN	*[groaning]* Oh no, not plan B, our Nat.

60

WALTER	You know we always get headaches when we go onto rewind.
DAN	Ah, that's right. It's an awful long rewind too ... all them years ago.
NATHAN	Sorry lads, it's part of our jobs. If they won't listen, we've just got to show them.
WALTER AND DAN	Oh all right, I suppose it's got to be done.

[They stand in a line facing the audience and press the tops of their heads with their index fingers. At the same time, NATHAN calls out 'Rewind' ... The three shepherds then exit the set by walking backwards in step. After a short pause, and from the opposite side of the set, three other shepherds enter, again walking backwards until they reach centre stage where they stop, forming quarter of a circle facing the audience. WALTER, DAN, and NATHAN re-enter still walking backwards, and join the others, thus forming half a circle facing the audience. All the shepherds then press the tops of their heads with their index fingers, while NATHAN shouts 'Play', and almost immediately the shepherds break into song to the tune of, 'We saw three ships'.]

ALL SHEPHERDS   *[with as much gusto as possible]*
'We saw three sheep go floating by,
on Noah's Ark, on Noah's Ark,
We saw three sheep go floating by,
On Noah's Ark, Friday morning ...

And what were on those sheep, all
   three,

On Noah's Ark, on Noah's Ark?
A hundred and forty thousand fleas,
On Noah's Ark, Friday morn . . .

[They are interrupted by the entrance of an ANGEL dressed as a choirboy.]

4TH SHEPHERD Oo, er. What's that? . . . He do look like that Aled Jones . . .

[or another famous choirboy]

[All the shepherds panic at this point, and run to hide in various places around the set. There are cries of: 'Oh no, anything but that' . . . 'Spare us, spare us' . . . 'Please don't sing' . . . 'Cover your ears everyone' . . .]

ANGEL *[in disgust]* I am not Aled Jones but an angel.

[The shepherds filter back with sighs of relief.]

. . . I have come to tell you the good news that to you this day, in the town of Bethlehem, a Saviour is born. He is the Christ. If you go now, you will find him wrapped in strips of cloth, and lying in a manger.

[The angel exits. The shepherds remain quiet for a while. The silence is broken by NATHAN.]

NATHAN Right then, I'm off. This I gotta see. *[In awe]*

. . . The Saviour of the world . . . Yep, I'm all for that. Who's coming then?

WALTER *[stepping forward]* I'd like to come, if that's all right by you.

DAN Yeah, and I.

NATHAN	*[to the three remaining]* 'Ow about you three then?
4TH SHEPHERD	*[doubtfully]* I dunno ... Me and the lads ought to 'ave a discussion over this ...

[The three doubting shepherds get together in a huddle and discuss in an animated way for a few seconds before turning back.]

... We ... that's the lads and me. We reckon you've been had. We reckon that bloke was Aled Jones. He was pullin' your legs, that's all. Anyhow, we've decided to stay here. If you want to go making fools of yourselves that's up to you.

NATHAN	That's your final say, is it?
4TH SHEPHERD	That's our final say, innit lads?
5TH AND 6TH SHEPHERDS	Ar ... Ar ...
NATHAN	Right, come on then, lads ...

[All the shepherds now line up at the front. All put index fingers to the tops of their heads. NATHAN shouts, 'Forward'. Simultaneously, the 4TH SHEPHERD cries, 'Rewind'. NATHAN's group now exit by turning and marching forwards off the set. The other group march off the set in the opposite direction, and backwards.

The scene at the stable is now constructed in as simple a way as possible. JOSEPH can enter with two chairs. He is followed by MARY holding the BABY. They take their places just as NATHAN, WALTER and DAN enter and pay homage to the child. After a suitable interval, JOSEPH

	indicates that the shepherds should leave.
	In doing so, the shepherds just move to
	the front of the acting area while JOSEPH,
	MARY *and the* BABY *exit.]*
NATHAN	*[in awe]* The Saviour of the world. There'll be no going back now, lads. ... In fact, we'd better go on fast forward to get back to those people we left behind in the future.
WALTER	How can you leave someone behind in the future, Nathan?
NATHAN	*[impatiently]* Well I don't know, do I? It's something to do with Einstein's theory of relationships ... I think ... *[exasperated]* Look, if you keep asking awkward questions like that, it's you I'll be leaving behind in future. Come on, back to the future.
	[They all press the tops of their heads again, and NATHAN *says,* 'Fast forward'. *The shepherds now run off the set. After a short pause they re-enter, still running, and looking suitably exhausted from their 'time travel'.]*
NATHAN	*[catching his breath]* Well ... there you are, ladies and gentlemen ... that's what happened ...
DAN	Hang on, Nat, you've missed out the important bit.
NATHAN	Which bit's that?
DAN	*[chiding him]* Oh come on, it's what we were given.
NATHAN	*[realising]* Oh my goodness, what a thing to forget! Show 'em your bits of paper, lads ...
	[The shepherds each produce rolls of

parchment tied with different coloured
ribbon. NATHAN *reads his to the audience.]*

'This is to certify that Nathan the
shepherd will one day be with me in
heaven' . . .

DAN   Can we show them what else we got,
Nathan?

NATHAN   Yes, all right.

             [DAN runs off, and returns with three
             crowns. They all place the crowns on
             their heads and proudly turn to the
             audience.]

WALTER   *[to the audience]* We got these as soon as
we knew he was the Saviour of the
world. Some other people came visit-
ing after us, but they'd already got
theirs.

             [As the shepherds start to exit WALTER
             says to DAN]

WALTER   Can I try yours on, Dan, see if it fits?

DAN   You've got your own crown, Walter
. . . I don't know, never satisfied with
what you've got, are you?

NATHAN   I don't suppose many of us will be in
this life, our Dan . . .

8

The Tea Party

Cast: MAD HATTER
                      ALICE
                      MARCH HARE
                      DORMOUSE

The MAD HATTER, *the* MARCH HARE, *and the* DORMOUSE *are all seated around the table when* ALICE *enters. The* DORMOUSE *is asleep.*

MAD HATTER	Take a seat, why don't you?
ALICE	I don't mind if I do.
MARCH HARE	One lump or five?
ALICE	But I haven't had any tea yet!
MAD HATTER	Don't be silly, she hasn't had any tea yet ... Dormouse, pour out some tea.
	[The DORMOUSE *wakes and tips the kettle into the* MARCH HARE's *lap. The* MARCH HARE *responds by jumping up and running round the table in pain. The* MAD HATTER *takes no notice. The* DORMOUSE *returns to his slumbers.]*
MAD HATTER	*[to Alice]* And how did you find us, pray?
ALICE	I just walked through my looking glass.
MARCH HARE	I did that once, very painful it was too ... My nose was up for weeks afterwards.
MAD HATTER	Would you like a fortune cookie? They

help to tell you all about the future, you know ... Or perhaps a currant bun, if you want to know what's happening to you now?

ALICE   Well, it might be good to know what's happening to me now, as I'm sure I don't quite understand all of this!

MAD HATTER   Dormouse, pass a currant bun to our guest.

                  [The DORMOUSE wakes and repeats his action with the kettle. The MARCH HARE runs around the table in pain again.]

ALICE   Oh dear, this is all very confusing. I don't know whether I'm coming or going!

MAD HATTER   Ha! *You* don't know whether you're coming or going? Tweedle Dum and Tweedle Dee are always pulling each other in opposite directions, the March Hare is for ever coming and going, though where from and where to, even he doesn't know. I seem to pass my day trying to sell hats at jumble sales in between throwing tea parties. *[Glaring at the sleeping DORMOUSE]* I never seem to receive any tea at these parties, however ... And he *[indicating the DORMOUSE]* ... doesn't come or go anywhere of note. It's all very boring.

ALICE   Why do you think it's all very boring?

MARCH HARE   It's all my fault, I'm afraid. I put the instruction book down somewhere, and I can't for the life of me remember where I left it.

ALICE   Is that all? Can't you remember what was written in it?

MARCH HARE   No, it was too big to remember all of it. It

	would have taken a lifetime to understand it all.
ALICE	Oh dear, what was it called?
DORMOUSE	*[sleepily]* 'How to make tea.'
MAD HATTER	Oh don't be so silly. It was called, 'How to organise jumble sales.'
MARCH HARE	I thought it was called, 'How to run a marathon and do the high jump.'
ALICE	We've got an instruction book where I come from. I don't suppose it would exist in a world of make believe like this. It's called the Bible.
ALL THREE TOGETHER	Never heard of it.

9

The Estate Agent, or 'I'm OK, Ya'

An Estate Agent? Or could there be a *Fall* in the value of property?!

Cast: JEREMY
          FELICITY

Inside an estate agent's. In the centre of the set is a table on top of which is a picnic basket. A notice to the front of the table reads 'Estate Agent, please take a card.' A couple enter, obviously yuppies.

JEREMY   This looks like the place, Felicity.
FELICITY   Yes, take a card, Jeremy.
JEREMY   *[takes a card and reads short-sightedly]* . . . 'Please address your requests to the basket.'
FELICITY   You are silly, Jeremy, put your glasses on. *[Pointing]* The basket's on the table.
JEREMY   Oh, right you are.
           [He dons glasses and leans on the table to address the basket.]
           Now, we were just wondering . . .
           [turning back to FELICITY]
           . . . I feel a dreadful twit you know, Flis, talking to a picnic basket like this.
FELICITY   Never mind, dear, I'm sure you're doing the right thing.

JEREMY   *[hesitates, but turns back to the basket]* We were
           wondering if you could help us? . . .
           [He giggles and turns to FELICITY.]
           Do you think it's going to talk back in a minute?

FELICITY   Don't be silly, Jeremy, just do as the card
           says.

JEREMY   Yes, dear. *[To the basket]* Uh, I'm looking for a
           suitable residence for my wife and myself. Uh,
           do you think you could help?
           [Long silence.]
           It's not saying anything, Flis. *[He giggles.]*

FELICITY   I can hear something, it's quite clear to me.

JEREMY   *[looking around him]* Where from?

FELICITY   From the basket, silly!

JEREMY   Oh, really?

FELICITY   A voice from the basket, yes. *[She looks puzzled]*
           Where've I heard that voice before? It's very
           familiar.

JEREMY   Are you feeling all right?

FELICITY   Do you mean to say you can't hear? . . . *[the
           voice, which only FELICITY can hear, interrupts from
           the basket]* . . . What? . . . Oh! *[to JEREMY]* I've got
           to do all the talking *[she goes to stand between
           JEREMY and the basket, and listens]* . . . Hmm? *[to
           JEREMY]* . . . It wants a bit more information.
           [She gets closer to the table]
           We're looking for a place with a large garden
           . . . No, just a small residence, but we do like
           the odd spot of gardening . . . fruit trees mostly
           . . . Oh really? What a coincidence . . . *[she
           suddenly looks embarrassed]* We haven't actually
           got a current address . . . First time buyers,
           that's right. Last place we had was a long term
           lease . . . *[she turns to JEREMY]* It wants to know
           why we left the last place. Shall I tell it the
           landlord threw a strop?

JEREMY	How can you say that?
FELICITY	It's true, isn't it?
JEREMY	Course it's not, not altogether anyhow. He threw us out for what happened.
FELICITY	Because we picked his fruit you mean?
JEREMY	It was written into the tenancy agreement that we leave that area of the property alone. Anyway, what do you mean we? It was you that did it.
FELICITY	Let's not go into all that again. *[She walks past JEREMY. He now walks over to the basket.]*
JEREMY	Now look here, we've seen a nice little number in *Country Life* which we quite like the look of, and ... *[he turns away in disgust]* I absolutely refuse to talk to a basket any more.
FELICITY	It's not just any old basket though, is it?
JEREMY	So what's so special about that basket?
FELICITY	*[opening the lid of the basket and looking inside]* Oh, isn't he lovely? Jeremy, do take a look.
JEREMY	*[glancing into the basket and turning away]* This is all getting a little too much for me. Put the lid down, Flis. I think we ought to be leaving.
FELICITY	Wait a sec' ... *[she bends close to the basket and grasps his hand]* ... Jeremy, it can talk, it's him that's doing the talking, not the basket. He wants to go with us. He says he knows of a really nice, centrally-placed residence. Everything we could hope for.
JEREMY	We had everything we could hope for in the last place.
FELICITY	Oh Jeremy, we couldn't exactly do everything we wanted, could we? *[She picks up the basket]* Come on. He's telling us how to get to this new place.
JEREMY	We can't just walk out of here with someone else's property!

73

FELICITY   He says he's ours now, and he'll stay with us
            for as long as we want him. Isn't that nice? . . . A
            snake in a basket! Think what our friends will
            say.

JEREMY   *[as they exit]* Oh, all right . . . I'm not really sure
            about the snake, you know. If the inside of the
            basket wasn't so dark and I wasn't so short-
            sighted, I'd be able to tell the breed of the thing.
            It might be a dangerous species, have you
            stopped to think of that?

FELICITY   *[stopping]* Can you hear someone laughing
            somewhere?

JEREMY   No, dear.

FELICITY   *[lifts the basket to listen before shrugging]*
            Must be imagining it. Come on. . . .
                [They exit.]

10

Jonah Takes a Dive

Cast:
   1ST NARRATOR
   2ND NARRATOR
   JONAH
   1ST SAILOR
   2ND SAILOR
   OTHER SAILORS

1ST NARRATOR   There once lived a man called Jonah . . .
      [JONAH enters wearing a sou-wester or raincoat.]

2ND NARRATOR   . . . who everyone knew as a loner.

1ST NARRATOR   *[giving the other a withering look]* You agreed not to rhyme it.

2ND NARRATOR   Sorry!

1ST NARRATOR   Anyway . . . *[continuing]* Jonah was given a message by God to go and tell the people of Nineveh . . .

2ND NARRATOR   . . . that they should stop doing what they shouldn't be doing, and do the things that they should be doing.

1ST NARRATOR   *[looking lost]* It says *repent* in my script.

2ND NARRATOR   Same thing.

1ST NARRATOR   Can we stick to the known way?

2ND NARRATOR   Righto.

1ST NARRATOR   So what did Jonah do?

2ND NARRATOR	Not what he was told, naughty boy.
1ST NARRATOR	He did the opposite.
2ND NARRATOR	Got on a boat . . .
	[Three SAILORS enter and join JONAH, form-ing a line facing the audience.]
1ST NARRATOR	Paddled his own canoe . . .
ALL SAILORS	*[in unison, protesting]* Fishing boat.
1ST NARRATOR	Figuratively speaking . . .
2ND NARRATOR	. . . and headed straight out of town in the opposite direction.
1ST NARRATOR	Where a storm was waiting for them.
	[During each whoosh from the narrators in turn, the crew of the ship lean sideways and stagger, as one, to the side of the acting area, giving the appearance of going with the roll of a ship.]
2ND NARRATOR	WHOOSH
1ST NARRATOR	WHOOSH
1ST SAILOR	I've never known a night like it!
OTHER SAILORS	He's never known a night like it!
2ND NARRATOR	WHOOSH
1ST NARRATOR	WHOOSH
2ND NARRATOR	WHHH until . . .
	[This catches the SAILORS unawares, as they are just starting to lean with the roll of the ship. One falls over.]
1ST SAILOR	*[annoyed, to 2ND NARRATOR]* Now look what you've done!
JONAH	*[coming to the rescue of the NARRATOR]* No, no, it was me what done it, er . . . who did it.
1ST NARRATOR	*[glaring at the 2ND NARRATOR and throw-ing part of the script over his shoulder]* until Jonah confessed that it was because of him that God had brought on the storm.
JONAH	Yes, right, my fault.

1ST NARRATOR	So he told the sailors to throw him overboard.
JONAH	*[horrified]* I did?
1ST NARRATOR	So they did.
	[The SAILORS pick JONAH up.]
JONAH	*[remembering]* So I did!
	[The SAILORS carry him off the set where they all shout.]
SAILORS OFF	Sperlash!
	[The SAILORS re-enter.]
1ST SAILOR	Lads, I reckon he'll be lonely out there at the mercy of the sea. What's say we give him some company?
2ND SAILOR	Good idea.
	[They all grab the 2ND NARRATOR and carry him off set.]
SAILORS OFF	Sperlash!
1ST NARRATOR	And the boat went on to its destination leaving Jonah to be swallowed up by a big fish . . .
	[The SAILORS walk backwards across the set in single file, each pretending to stroke an oar through the water. They exit.]
	. . . and the other narrator to be swallowed up by pride!
	[Pause]
	. . . Jonah was in the belly of the fish three days and nights.
JONAH	*(off)* I've never known three days or nights like it!
1ST NARRATOR	Until, on the third day, after he'd prayed to God for help, he was made to be sick . . . the fish, not Jonah.
VOICE OFF	*[Very deep and loud]*
	Oh no, I think I'm going to be . . . Groan!!!
	[Enter JONAH, soaking wet.]

1ST NARRATOR	Phwah!!! Stay over that side, you smell of old sardines. . . . And while you're over there, tell these people what lesson you've learnt from all this.
JONAH	Two lessons, really . . . The first is that if God wants you to do something, you've just got to do it. It'll only hurt if you try running away, or try doing it in your own time . . .
1ST NARRATOR	And what's the second lesson?
JONAH	It isn't half dark in the belly of a big fish!

11

Puppets

Cast: NARRATOR
              PUPPETS

The scene is the storeroom of a puppet theatre. A number of puppets are arranged around the room in a haphazard fashion, but with space around each. They appear to be suspended from above by single invisible strings which are connected in the first instance to the small of each puppet's back. Each puppet is therefore standing, bent double, and limp from the waist up.

NARRATOR   These puppets belong to the puppet master. He has owned them for many years and has often been heard to boast that he carved them from the finest wood. The reality is that he stole them from the greatest puppet maker of all time.

              The puppets wait in this room ready to perform for the master. When he comes for them he will attach strings as necessary to each puppet in turn . . .

              [Each PUPPET, *in a set pattern, now seems to have more invisible strings attached to one limb at a time. All the* PUPPETS *become upright with arms outstretched. It can be seen that one or two of the* PUPPETS *are blindfolded.]*

              . . . They are now ready to face the world and

perform when the puppet master requires them . . .

[One of the PUPPETS *which has remained lying flat on the ground now slowly stands. He has no strings.]*

. . . But one of the figures is special. Although inside the puppet master's storeroom, this figure has never performed for the puppet master. It can never belong to him. The puppet master has often tried to make the figure dance for him. Pierced holes in the figure's hands and feet stand as evidence to the fact. But this figure needs no strings to guide him. He is guided by a divine spirit . . .

[The figure now moves freely among the PUPPETS.*]*

. . . This figure, which was carved from living wood by the puppet maker, has been sent to the master's storeroom to set the other puppets free . . .

[The figure now goes to each PUPPET *in turn. Avoiding those blindfolded, he passes his hand over the tops of each* PUPPET. *This action severs the strings of the* PUPPETS, *and they collapse one by one to the floor. Only the blindfolded* PUPPETS *remain standing.]*

. . . He gives them power to live a life of freedom . . .

[The figure now stands at the front of the PUPPETS, *and lifts his arms. One by one the* PUPPETS *who were lying on the ground come to life and, becoming aware of their freedom and new found life, go to each other and embrace. After a while, the figure walks off the set at the back and the* PUPPETS *with new life follow. One*

PUPPET *loiters after the others have left. He looks around him at the blindfolded* PUPPETS *and then off set to those who are free.*]

... And what of those remaining, you ask yourself? ... Just watch!

[*The uncertain* PUPPET *eventually turns slowly back to the blindfolded* PUPPETS *and, walking over to the nearest, strokes its face and arms gently. It then takes a piece of cloth from the pocket of the blindfolded* PUPPET *and, going back to its original position in the room, ties the cloth around its own eyes. It immediately slumps forward from the waist, and becomes a* PUPPET *once more.*]

... Some would say that it is far easier to remain a puppet. Those who have eyes to see, let them see.

12

It's Hard on the Streets

Cast: FRANK SHOVEL
           SHABBY MAN
           WELL DRESSED MAN
           TWO MUGGERS
           PRIEST
           CITY MAN
           SAM SAMARITAN

A street corner in the windy city. FRANK SHOVEL *enters wearing a raincoat and Homburg. He is a newspaper reporter.*

FRANK   The name's Shovel, Frank Shovel. I'm a
           reporter with the *Tribune*. . . . Used to be
           an eye, private eye that is. But it was hard
           being a private eye on the streets of the
           city . . . would've been even harder if I'd
           been a cat's eye . . . but that's another
           story . . . What I'm gonna tell you now
           happened a few weeks back . . . It was a
           cold night, so cold the icicles hanging
           from the fender of the car were playing a
           melody as I drove over ruts in the road. I
           couldn't quite pick out the tune, my mind
           was elsewhere. I was onto a lead, some-
           thing hot. I knew if I kept my nose to the
           ground and didn't get my fingers burnt,

I'd end up with a blister on my nostril . . . I didn't care, I was after one man. I wanted to find him. See why he did what he did . . . You wanna know why I was so interested in this particular guy? Okay, I'll show ya. What follows are the events that led up to my drive downtown that night.

[He exits. Two men enter from either side of the set. They both wear heavy clothing to protect against the cold. One is well dressed, the other has shabbier clothing. The latter side-steps in front of the well-dressed man, barring his way.]

SHABBY MAN   Ya got a light, mac?

WELL DRESSED MAN   *[English accent]* No, I'm terribly sorry, this is the only overcoat I possess actually . . .

[At this point, two men rush on from behind him, and proceed to mug and rob the man of his money and overcoat. They are accomplices to the SHABBY MAN, and as they exit they divide the 'spoils' between them. They leave the man on his knees, clutching his stomach. FRANK SHOVEL re-enters.]

FRANK   Okay, the scene's set, the guy's lying there. He's wondering how he can see the stars in the gutter . . . The stars go out, one by one.

[The man slowly collapses on to his side, unconscious. FRANK exits . . . Enter, a PRIEST.]

PRIEST   *[stepping around the body]* Dear God, another one. The weakness of men, to hit the bottle like this. [To the man] Get up, man. Haven't you got a wife and children to go home to? Where's your self respect?

[He exits, and after a short pause, a well

dressed CITY MAN *enters. He also walks around the body of the man.]*

CITY MAN   It's about time the President passed a law about these tramps. Damned vagrants ought to be locked up out of the way!

[He exits. FRANK *re-enters and stands over the body.]*

FRANK   Okay, the guy's had doors shut in his face before. But never like this. His lights have been put out and his anti-freeze is disappearing down the drain. He's on his way to the scrap heap . . .

*[*FRANK *steps back, as a man well wrapped against the cold enters. The man stops immediately beside the man on the ground and, helping him to his feet, they both exit.* FRANK *steps forward again.]*

. . . That's the guy I was after. He'd acted strange, out of context. He didn't do what most men do. What I heard later was that he'd gone out of his way to take the man to hospital. Even left money with the duty nurse to cover expenses. As a human interest story I could see it stretched across the front page of my Daily. 'Man rescued from junk heap by hero' . . . Three or four days later, I got the break I needed. I took that drive I told you about. The information was to lead me to a downtown ethnic minority area. That's where I met up with Sam . . . Sam Samaritan . . .

[He turns sideways and, walking a few paces, takes a notebook from his pocket. SAM SAMARITAN *walks on from opposite.]*

. . . Okay, Sam, you did what you did.

85

	What did you expect to get out of it at the end of the day?
SAM	The reward of knowing I did it for a neighbour.
FRANK	Now just a minute, the guy was too rich to be coming from this sort of neighbourhood.
SAM	Oh, you got it wrong. We're all neighbours on this earth, especially in God's eyes. When I found him, he was more of a neighbour than most I can name. I've been in that gutter and I know how cold it can be ... Maybe not as cold as him, though. The man was helpless, he had no money, no identity ... Oh yes, he was my neighbour all right ...

[SAM exits. FRANK turns back to the audience, pocketing his notebook.]

| FRANK | End of story! As I drove back uptown I knew the story wouldn't get into print. The editor wouldn't buy it. He wanted sensation, and this was too good to be true. The *Tribune* readers wouldn't identify with it. We were out to sell copy, and this sort of story..? Well, maybe it would sell elsewhere, but I couldn't use it ... |

Like I say, it's hard out there on the streets of the city. My job is to get out there and report it.

13

One Flew Over the Church Spire

If Christ were born today, in a world where money is everything to many people, how would he be welcomed at a modern inn?

Cast:
           PROPRIETOR
           JOSEPH
           MARY
           BELL-BOY
           3 SHEPHERDS
           3 KINGS

The scene is a hotel lobby. At the back of the set is a large clock which shows three o'clock. A well dressed hotel proprietor is on duty and is writing, when a poorly dressed couple enter. The woman is pregnant.

PROPRIETOR	*[looking them up and down]* Yes?
JOSEPH	Have you a room for us overnight? We've tried other places, but everywhere is full. We've had a long journey and my wife is expecting our first child at any moment.
PROPRIETOR	*[curtly]* Out of the question. Full up.
JOSEPH	Anywhere would do, my wife must rest.
PROPRIETOR	There's a lock-up garage at the back if you're that desperate. As long as you don't tell anyone of course. Don't want all

the vagrants around here cottoning on, do we?

[The PROPRIETOR rings a bell and a BELL-BOY appears.]

PROPRIETOR	Show these people where number three is, round the back.
BELL-BOY	Room number three, right you are.
PROPRIETOR	No, garage three. We've no room in the main building. You do know where the garages are, don't you?
BELL-BOY	*[embarrassed]* Yes, sir, of course, sir. *[To JOSEPH]* If you'd like to follow me.

[They exit. To indicate the passing of time, the PROPRIETOR now walks to the back of the set and puts the clock forward five hours. He then returns to the desk just as three men enter, dressed as SHEPHERDS.]

PROPRIETOR	*[taken aback]* What the . . .?
1ST SHEPHERD	We're lookin' for the King.
PROPRIETOR	I beg your pardon?
2ND SHEPHERD	The King, we're lookin' fer 'im.
PROPRIETOR	Well, I'm sorry but we've no royalty of any description booked in here tonight.
3RD SHEPHERD	He's hardly likely to be booked in. He's only due to see the first light of day tonight.

[The other SHEPHERDS look at him with a strained expression.]

1ST SHEPHERD	You trying to confuse the issue, or something? 'Ow can anyone see the light of day at night, you stupid shepherd?
PROPRIETOR	If you're trying to tell me that you expect to find a baby on the premises, I can tell you right now . . .

[The BELL-BOY rushes in.]

BELL-BOY	Excuse me, sir, but I thought you should

88

	know that the woman in garage three has given birth to a son. The hotel doctor's there now.
1ST SHEPHERD	No babies on the premises eh? C'mon, that's what we're here for, lads. *[To the BELL-BOY]* Where's this 'ere lock up?
BELL-BOY	*[stammering]* Well ... you can hardly miss it, there's a strange light from the sky lighting up the whole of the garage and the forecourt.
1ST SHEPHERD	*[decisively]* Good enough for us. Sounds like the place, doesn't it, lads?

[The SHEPHERDS make for the exit, followed closely by the BELL-BOY.]

You'd better go in front, lad, and show us the way. *[Exit]*

[The PROPRIETOR stares at the door for a few seconds, then walks across to look out.]

| PROPRIETOR | *[sarcastically calling out]* Excuse me ... You wouldn't mind doing me a small favour would you, on your way out? You wouldn't like to remove your flock of sheep from the outer foyer? Yes ... Thank you so much ... And boy, when you come back, find a dustpan and brush from somewhere, if it's not too inconvenient ... thank you so much. |

[He returns to the desk saying]

... the day started so well, too.

[Pause]

[The PROPRIETOR now goes to the clock at the back of the set and resets the clock to eleven o'clock before resuming his place behind the desk. The BELL-BOY re-enters breathlessly.]

| BELL-BOY | *[rushing his words]* It's gone crazy out |

there. You can't get near lock-up three, all
the sheep are blocking the way, and . . .
and . . . well, all the sky's lit up, and
there's all sorts of strange things going
on, and . . . and . . .

> [The PROPRIETOR is now looking at the BELL-
> BOY with a worldly-wise expression, which
> causes the boy to continue lamely.]

. . . well, you won't believe it until you see
it for yourself.

PROPRIETOR   [quietly, with a fixed grin] I believe you,
now just calm down and tell me what else
you'd have me believe.

BELL-BOY   It's incredible I know, but there's loads of
UFOs flying around out there. They're
just flying round the heavens and sort of
[lamely] . . . well, singing.

PROPRIETOR   That's nice, is it a pretty sound?

BELL-BOY   [ecstatic] Oh yes, it's beautiful, you should
hear it for yourself.

PROPRIETOR   And what do these UFOs look like, hmm?

BELL-BOY   Well, not like what you always hear about
. . . They're what I'd imagine angels to
look like, only brighter, and you can make
out wings too . . . I think. Can't make out
too much detail . . . I was standing out the
front just now and you should have seen
it, one came over really low and flew
round the side of the building, another
one came in low over the church.

PROPRIETOR   [suddenly angry] Look, I don't know how
far you intend to take this rubbish, but . . .

> [At that moment, three KINGS enter wearing
> traditional clothing.]

1ST KING   We have come from the far east in search
of the new born King.

90

2ND KING	We have brought him gifts of gold, rare frankincense and myrrh.
PROPRIETOR	Oh right, I see, it's a game of charades. Well, I think you'll find that the King has other visitors at the moment, in fact quite a few visitors. If you don't mind waiting in line behind a flock of sheep, some shepherds, and lots of UFOs, you'll find them all round the back, in lock-up three. *[Dismissively]* Follow the pretty lights, you can't miss the party . . . Oh, and if you've got any camels, please don't leave them in the foyer, we've had enough trouble with sheep as it is.

[The KINGS exit and the BELL-BOY turns to go.]

. . . Not you.

BELL-BOY	*[turning]* Sir?
PROPRIETOR	Leave your uniform downstairs and pick up a week's wages on your way out. Tell the personnel office to advertise your post in the local press. That's all. Close the door on your way out.

[The BELL-BOY exits. The PROPRIETOR now puts the clock forward nine hours to eight o'clock next day. As he returns to his desk, enter MARY holding the baby, with JOSEPH.]

. . . Oh, it's you. You should have been here last night, you know. We had a rare old party. Everyone was having a great time at my expense. People dressed up as shepherds. There were sheep, angels on camels, bell-boys on the hop. One flew over the church spire, one flew over the cuckoo's nest. Oh, it was a joy to behold.

Funny lights in the sky. You name it, we had it. Even kings, yes, we even had kings. Of course, it was all a practical joke. Won't catch me falling for that sort of thing.

JOSEPH *[smiling]* How much do we owe you?

PROPRIETOR Rental of a garage for one night? Uh, let's call it three shekels, shall we?

JOSEPH *[handing over a coin]* Would you accept that?

PROPRIETOR *[looking at it closely]* What is it?

JOSEPH A gold coin.

PROPRIETOR Doesn't look like it to me.

JOSEPH There's a mark on it to prove it's made from the purest of gold.

PROPRIETOR *[turning it over while MARY and JOSEPH exit]* Nothing here except a cross on one side . . . doesn't mean a thing to me.

> *[He looks up to see that he is talking to himself, shrugs, pockets the coin and walks off.]*

14

Castle Heart

What happens when the human spirit is confronted by the message of Christianity? 'Castle Heart' explores some of the barriers which some may erect as a defence to that message.

Cast:
JUDGE
ADVOCATE
VOICE OFF
KING SELF
CORPORAL I DON'T KNOW
SERGEANT I DON'T CARE
CAPTAIN PUTITOV
WILL

The scene is a court room. A JUDGE *and an* ADVOCATE *are present. To one side is a witness stand, and a chair is placed beside the witness stand.*

JUDGE Right, let's have the first one, shall we? The sooner we start, the sooner I can get to my sherry luncheon with the inner circle.

ADVOCATE Very well, your honour. The first case of the day is a civil action brought by one King Self against King Jesus.

JUDGE Bit meaty first thing, isn't it? Oh well, can't choose the order they come in, I

	suppose. *[Nods assent to the* ADVOCATE*]* Right.
ADVOCATE	*[calling off]* Call King Self.
VOICE OFF	Call King Self.
	*[*KING SELF *enters and takes his place on the witness stand. He is the archetypal 'upper class twit'.]*
ADVOCATE	*[handing him a book]* Repeat after me . . .
KING SELF	*[interrupting]* . . . After me.
ADVOCATE	No, no, no, I promise to tell the truth, the whole truth, and nothing but the truth.
KING SELF	*[patting him gently on the head with the book]* Then you must be a source of constant pleasure to your mother. *[To the* JUDGE*]* Isn't it nice to know that there are still a few honest commoners in the world?
JUDGE	*[smiling inanely]* I think we'd better proceed to the next question.
ADVOCATE	You are bringing an action against one King Jesus, for the return of what you state is your rightful property, is that correct?
KING SELF	Course it is, old chap. Everyone knows that Castle Heart has been in my family for yonks.
ADVOCATE	Would you tell us, in your own words, what happened on the day you lost Castle Heart.
KING SELF	Deceived all the way down the line, wasn't I? I mean, for a kick orf, I was told that a big army was going to invade the land, so what do I go and do? Build three outer walls as extra defence to the Castle, that's what I go and do! Waste of money, time and energy as it turns out . . . Big army indeed!
ADVOCATE	I believe you gave names to these walls?
KING SELF	Just a little whim of mine, doncha know. Other great things have been named after their designers, haven't they? I mean, there's

	the Eiffel Tower named after Mister Eiffel . . . Big Ben was named after the flowerpot men, so why not have the walls named after my best soldiers?
JUDGE	Uh, would you mind telling the court the events on the day you were thrown out of Castle Heart?
KING SELF	Let's see now. I went to bed for my afternoon nap as usual thinking everything was all right, everything locked up and safe, and so on. And when I woke up, I'd lost everything. It's as simple as that really. All my men had betrayed me, and I was being pushed out of the back door of my property.
JUDGE	[to ADVOCATE] Have we any witnesses to throw any light on the proceedings?
ADVOCATE	Yes, your honour.
JUDGE	[to KING SELF] You may step down, your majesty. [To the ADVOCATE] Call the next witness, if you don't mind. Perhaps things will start falling into place as we go on.
ADVOCATE	[after KING SELF has seated himself in the spare chair] Call Corporal I don't know.
VOICE OFF	Call Corporal I don't know.
	[The CORPORAL enters and takes his place on the stand. He is a cockney.]
ADVOCATE	You are the officer-in-charge of the first line of defence at Castle Heart, are you not? The first line being the outer wall of three, known as 'The wall of Ignorance'?
CORPORAL	'S right, named after me, wannit?
ADVOCATE	Quite! Tell us what happened that day, the day King Self was forced to leave the Castle.
CORPORAL	For a start, he wasn't forced to leave the Castle. His right hand man told me that.

ADVOCATE	His right hand man being?
CORPORAL	His name's Will.
ADVOCATE	*[to the JUDGE]* One of our later witnesses, your honour. *[To the CORPORAL]* So what happened to you that day?
CORPORAL	I was patrolling the wall as usual, wasn't I?, looking for signs of an attack from this army we'd been told to expect. So this 'ere solitary geezer comes up to the gate, and bold as brass asks to be let in!
ADVOCATE	Did you know who this er, geezer was?
CORPORAL	Turned out to be King Jesus, dinnit? Anyhow, we has this chat you see, about life and suchlike, and I finds him to be a really nice bloke. More than that really. He was what you might call too nice for this world, if you get my drift.
ADVOCATE	And you let him in through the gate?
CORPORAL	Course I did, I'd never heard the like of what he had to say to me, and I wanted to hear more, didn't I?
ADVOCATE	Thank you, you may step down. *[To the JUDGE, as CORPORAL exits]* I'd like to call the second witness, your honour.
JUDGE	Very well.
ADVOCATE	Call Sergeant I don't care.
VOICE OFF	Call Sergeant I don't care.
	[SERGEANT enters and takes the stand.]
ADVOCATE	Sergeant I don't care, you are in charge of the second wall, is that correct?
SERGEANT	The wall of indifference, that's right.
ADVOCATE	What happened on the day in question, Sergeant?
SERGEANT	The finest thing that could have happened to any castle ruled by a tyrant, I would have said.

96

[KING SELF jumps to his feet.]

KING SELF   I say, that's a bit thick, you know.

SERGEANT   Not half as thick as your dungeon walls, full of people who couldn't pay taxes. And not a quarter the thickness of your strongroom walls either. Not that that exists any more, now we've redistributed your wealth among the poor of the kingdom.

KING SELF   *[in a high pitched voice]* I beg your pardon?

SERGEANT   It was their money in the first place!

KING SELF   *[speechless]* Ubbu, ubbu, ubbu.

JUDGE   *[banging his gavel]* Order, order. This is a court of law, you know, not the House of Commons.

ADVOCATE   Thank you, your honour. *[To the SERGEANT]* What did you see on that day?

SERGEANT   This King Jesus turning up at the gate of my wall. He'd obviously made himself known at the wall of ignorance. Of course, it didn't matter to me who he was at the time, I'd been told to let no one past me, not even the poorest carpenter.

ADVOCATE   Then how did he get past you?

SERGEANT   I suppose it was the way he talked with me. From what he said it was obvious he cared for me, and for all people, no matter what faults they had. I'd never known that quality in a man before. Through the years I suppose I'd got used to having King Self running things for his own benefit. I could see I'd become quite indifferent about things around me. *[Pause]* If it had been you, and you knew someone cared for you, would you have turned that person away from your door?

ADVOCATE   I'm afraid I can't offer an opinion on that, but the court is here to consider your

97

	remarks. Thank you, Sergeant, you may step down.
	[The SERGEANT exits.]
KING SELF	It's all nonsense of course. I think the world of my subjects.
ADVOCATE	If it pleases your honour, I'd like to call the officer-in-charge of the final wall ... *[the JUDGE nods his assent]* ... Call Captain Putitov.
VOICE OFF	Call Captain Putitov.
	[The CAPTAIN enters and takes his place in the witness box.]
ADVOCATE	You have charge of the largest of the three walls, the Wall of Procrastination, am I right?
CAPTAIN	*[well spoken]* That is quite correct.
ADVOCATE	You were on duty the day King Jesus approached the wall?
CAPTAIN	Yes.
ADVOCATE	And you allowed him through?
CAPTAIN	Not at first I didn't. I was the highest ranking officer in the army at the time, and had my orders from King Self. It was up to me to show the soldiers under me a consistent pattern of leadership.
ADVOCATE	Then why did you weaken your position of authority by giving way to this King Jesus?
CAPTAIN	*[firmly]* The decision I made to open the gates to King Jesus was not due to weakness on my part.
ADVOCATE	Are you saying you did it to strengthen your position?
CAPTAIN	I am a soldier, sir, and have been one for as long as I can remember. I am used to giving and taking orders without question. On that particular day I was not expecting my life to

be turned upside down so emphatically. I was prepared to listen to this man because I realised he had managed to talk his way through the two outer walls, which only proved to me what I'd always feared, that ignorance and indifference can be overcome by earnest conversation. I was fascinated to know how he'd done it, and thought that if I showed interest to a degree, I'd find out. I felt that my strict training and discipline would stand up to any clever argument he might throw at me. So in conversation with him, I tried side-stepping any requests of his to pass through the gate by saying things like, 'Can't we talk about this tomorrow?' or, 'Let me think these things over.' I suppose I thought that he might eventually lose interest and go away. The remarkable thing about it all though, was that he had an answer for everything. He said things with such love and authority that my trying to put him off started to seem so ridiculous. I could easily have held a mirror up to myself and asked, 'Why are you throwing away a chance of knowing something good and true?'

ADVOCATE   What finally convinced you to open the gate?

CAPTAIN   Something he said which told me of the true nature of the man.

ADVOCATE   Which was?

CAPTAIN   He told me he'd once known a captain like myself. He'd asked this man time and again to allow him to be King in his life. The man had his own version of King Self in his life, a man who was a tyrant, and yet a man whom the Captain obeyed without question. Though he could see the wrong in his own king, the Captain couldn't bring himself to switch allegiance. His indecision was his complete and utter undoing.

ADVOCATE   What happened to him?

CAPTAIN   This other Captain, you mean?

ADVOCATE   Yes.

CAPTAIN   He died an unhappy man. He could never quite pluck up enough courage to change his life for the best by turning his back on his old king.

ADVOCATE   And so you opened the gate?

CAPTAIN   Yes, certainly not in a moment of weakness though. I knew it would mean a complete change of lifestyle, and so it's proved. A fighting soldier is not very often required in an atmosphere of peace and trust.

ADVOCATE   Thank you, you may step down.

[The CAPTAIN exits.]

The last witness, your honour, is Will, King Self's righthand man. *[Calling out]* Call Will.

VOICE OFF Call Will.

[WILL enters, and takes the stand.]

ADVOCATE   Will, you hold the keys to the main door of Castle Heart, is that correct?

WILL   That's correct, yes.

ADVOCATE   Would you say you know King Self better than most?

WILL   Yes, I suppose so.

ADVOCATE   What was he like as your King?

WILL   I felt sorry for him a lot of the time.

ADVOCATE   Why?

WILL   Because I knew that fear dominated his life. It controlled his selfish nature. He never got close to anybody because of his fear of love.

	He never understood anything other than what he could do with money. His life *was* his money.
ADVOCATE	And you did everything required of you as King Self's servant?
WILL	Up to a point.
ADVOCATE	Up to what point?
WILL	The point where King Jesus came to the door of Castle Heart. I didn't know which way to turn at first.
ADVOCATE	And why's that?
WILL	I'd had enough of the fear which kept King Self going, and there was a perfect King outside the Castle door, someone who promised freedom and a fresh understanding of life.
ADVOCATE	Then how were you torn between the two kings?
WILL	Mostly because King Self was the only king I'd ever known. Now I think of it, I suppose his fear had rubbed off on me. Ironic, isn't it, to think of being afraid of freedom and love?
ADVOCATE	What finally made you open the door of Castle Heart?
WILL	I don't think I ever would have, quite honestly, if it hadn't been for King Self losing his temper. He threatened that if I dared to touch the door handle he'd personally see to it that the life was crushed out of me. It was almost as if someone had lifted a great curtain from my eyes. I looked at King Self at that moment and saw real fear. I had to open the door, you see, I just couldn't be a part of the fear any more.
ADVOCATE	I have one last question for you, and it's an

	important one. Corporal I don't know states that King Self was not forced out of his own Castle. Is that correct?
KING SELF	*[jumping to his feet]* Course it's not correct. I was thrown out, lock, stock and barrel, wasn't I?
JUDGE	Sit down please, King Self. *[to WILL]* Answer the question if you please.
WILL	Nobody laid a finger on King Self, your honour. As soon as King Jesus set foot in Castle Heart, it was as though the whole place was suddenly filled with light and peace.
JUDGE	You're sure nobody threw King Self out?
WILL	As soon as King Jesus entered, King Self just appeared to become a stranger to the Castle and everybody in it. He quietly packed a big bag and left without a word.
ADVOCATE	That would seem an unusual move, wouldn't it?
WILL	I've thought about it a lot since, and there's only one reason I can think of which would explain why he went without a fight.
ADVOCATE	And what might that reason be?
WILL	That love, perfect love that is, is far stronger than fear.
	[There follows a long pause during which KING SELF stands and wordlessly exits.]
JUDGE	*[banging his gavel]* Case dismissed.

15

No Strings

Cast: 1ST VIOLINIST
                      2ND VIOLINIST

Enter two men. They are carrying violin cases.

1ST VIOLINIST   That was all I needed, to be put in the back row.

2ND VIOLINIST   The arrangement did call for the brass to be right up front. Can't argue with the composer, can you? I mean, he's got the final say, after all.

1ST VIOLINIST   Got to hand it to him, as a march it worked well.

2ND VIOLINIST   The timing was quite something too.

1ST VIOLINIST   Do you think the way it went down had anything to do with the conductor?

2ND VIOLINIST   In time to come, I think it'll probably be considered as the definitive interpretation of the composer's work.
[Pause]

1ST VIOLINIST   All the same, it did feel strange to be in the back row like that.

2ND VIOLINIST   Well, the reason for our position became evident during the seventh movement, didn't it?

1ST VIOLINIST   When the work reached its crescendo, you mean?

2ND VIOLINIST	The fanfare of trumpets was designed to round off the Jericho Symphony, you know.
	[Pause]
1ST VIOLINIST	*[awed]* And the roar that went up from the gallery when that sounded. Unbelievable, wasn't it?
2ND VIOLINIST	Someone said afterwards, they felt the earth move under their feet.
1ST VIOLINIST	Look how many trumpets they were using!
2ND VIOLINIST	*[thoughtful]* Mmm.
1ST VIOLINIST	Everything'll be back to normal for tonight though, won't it?
2ND VIOLINIST	Brass at the rear, do you mean?
1ST VIOLINIST	Yes.
2ND VIOLINIST	Oh don't worry about that, we'll be at the front again, that's a certainty.
1ST VIOLINIST	What is it we're doing tonight?
2ND VIOLINIST	The War Requiem.
1ST VIOLINIST	Ah ... *[pause]* ... You know something? I've never been more envious of the trumpet than I was tonight. What that instrument can do sometimes is quite devastating.
2ND VIOLINIST	If we all played the trumpet, the world would be a pretty boring place now, wouldn't it?
1ST VIOLINIST	Yes, I suppose you're right. We all have our talents ... *[pause]* ... Do you think it may be too presumptuous to expect that we could bring the house down tonight?
2ND VIOLINIST	How loudly can you blow the violin?

16

Sowing

The Parable of the Sower, told down the local street market?

Cast: SID
            HARRY
            1ST PLANT
            2ND PLANT
            3RD PLANT
            4TH PLANT

SID   Roll up, roll up, roll up, step right this way, ladies and gentlemen. Bend your ears my way a little as I tell you of a product which is guaranteed, yes, guaranteed to give you perfect returns for your time and effort ... and would you believe it, there is absolutely no money required to obtain this unique offer ... *[calls off]* Harry, would you be so kind as to bring out the demonstration pack.

HARRY   *[entering, and beckoning behind him]* Okay pack, out you come.
    [Enter four people dressed to look like flowers. They all wear a 'halo' of large petals, and each indicates varying degrees of shyness. They form a line facing the audience.]

| | There y'are, Sid, all spruce and tidy for the lovely people. |
| SID | Thank you, Harry, and may I say how nice our little pack are looking today. |

[The PLANTS show embarrassment and coyness. SID leans forward to the audience and says quietly]

Ladies and gentlemen . . .

[He now claps his hands and loudly states (making the PLANTS jump)]

We are here today to show you the remarkable *[clap hands]* the stupendous *[clap hands]* and yes . . . the miraculous results that you can achieve when you treat your plants to the wonder product which we are about to introduce to you today . . .

| HARRY | . . . What Sid's telling you about, ladies and gentlemen, has been tried and tested so many times, it defies logic . . . |
| SID | . . . And what is this wonder product that we're going overboard about, I hear you ask yourself? Well I'm going to tell you . . . after we put some of our plants through a few tests with other products which we've brought specially with us today. Harry, bring forward our first little guinea pig. |

[HARRY brings forward the 1ST PLANT.]

HARRY	Here we are, ladies and gentlemen, one hundred per cent, all healthy, and raring to go for our first test.
SID	But first we have to re-pot the plant.
1ST PLANT	*[taken aback]* Do what?!
HARRY	Sorry, Sid, you will forgive me, of course, a momentary lapse on my part. *[To the PLANT]* All right, take your shoes and socks off while I go and get the bowls.

[HARRY *exits as the* PLANT *protests.*]

SID You can't argue, you're a plant. It says on the side of the packet that we can put you in any compound we so desire.

[*He indicates to the other* PLANTS.]

The same goes for the rest of you. I want all your root systems exposed to the elements.

2ND PLANT [*as they all take off shoes and socks*] If we get frost bite, we'll know who to blame.

[HARRY *re-enters with four bowls which he places in front of the individual* PLANTS.]

SID Right, Harry, if you'd like to bring in our first treat for the lovely plant we have here.

[HARRY *exits and brings on a jug of water during the following.*]

Ladies and gentlemen, the plant before you is about to be subjected to an element fairly familiar to all of us here, and one which you will no doubt have heard of at some time during your working lives.

HARRY It's called the union element, and if we apply a small amount to our plant's root system . . .

[*he pours a little drop into the bowl*]

SID . . . You'll notice no adverse effects. But if we were to cover the entire root system with the union element? . . .

[HARRY *nonchalantly tips the contents of the jug into the bowl, whereupon the* 1ST PLANT *smiles briefly.*]

2ND PLANT This calls for an all-out strike brothers . . .

[*The* 1ST PLANT *now clutches its heart and dies.*]

SID Not a pretty sight, I think you'll agree, ladies and gentlemen . . . but wait, we haven't finished . . . Our next test is coming right up . . . Harry, number two plant.

HARRY [*bringing forward the* 2ND PLANT] As you see,

107

	another good sound plant for our second test.
2ND PLANT	*[adopting a 'Yuppie' accent]* I say, would you mind awfully if I opted out of this?
SID	Sorry my old flower, it's on your contract which is written ...
2ND PLANT AND SID	*[together]* ... on the side of the packet.

[Exit HARRY to fetch second jug.]

| SID | *[As 2ND PLANT steps into its bowl]* Now some of you will know that there are a few products on the market which offer quick results ... What do we think of these products? We're going to let you judge for yourselves ... |

[Enter HARRY with jug]

... Harry, if you wouldn't mind doing the honours?

[HARRY pours the contents into the bowl.]

| SID | It's a proprietary brand of quick-grow. Supposed to give you maximum growth in half the time. |

[2ND PLANT becomes very lively and starts beating its chest in a frantic imitation of Tarzan. In its last moments it leaps ape-like out of the bowl and collapses on the floor.]

| HARRY | Which only goes to prove that a plant with a fragile root structure just can't take force feeding ... Enough said? ... Sid. |
| SID | Right, two down, two to go ... Now I can hear some of you at the back saying, 'This is all new to me. I've never tried the union element or quick-grow ... All right, how about your common or garden, everyday elements? ... If we take our third plant ... |

[He beckons forward the 3RD PLANT who

immediately *produces a placard which reads:*
'Ban experiments on live plants'.]

... Oh, I see, a silent protest ...

[3RD PLANT shrugs, discards the placard and moves forward to stand in its bowl while HARRY exits.]

... The first thing Harry's going to add to the plant's root system is ...

[HARRY re-enters carrying an ash tray full of cigarette butts.]

... Ashes ...

[HARRY empties the contents of the ash tray into the bowl and exits again. The 3RD PLANT now has a coughing fit. HARRY re-enters carrying a glass of beer.]

HARRY   I shall now add to the plant another common element, essence of fermented barley.

[He pours the beer into the bowl and exits again. 3RD PLANT now reels drunkenly and continues coughing.]

SID   ... And last, but not least, ladies and gentlemen ...

[HARRY enters carrying a simple document.]

... We have Income Tax extract ...

[HARRY drops the form into the bowl.]

3RD PLANT   Oh well, that's it. This puts too much of a demand on me.

[curls up and dies]

SID   Nothing more to be said on that one, is there, Harry?

HARRY   Not really, our Sid.

SID   Which brings us neatly to the last one, eh Harry?

HARRY   I suppose so, Sid.

SID   If you'd like to get the, uh ...

HARRY   Will do, Sid.

109

	[He exits.]
SID	As for our fourth plant, ladies and gentlemen ...
	[He beckons the worried 4TH PLANT forward.] ... he need have no worries. *[With a sense of relief, 4TH PLANT steps into its bowl just as HARRY returns with a jug of plain water.]*
HARRY	This is it, ladies and gentlemen. It's free, and it's yours for the asking. It's called 'My Word' solution. Just that, 'My Word'. *[He pours the water into the bowl. The 4TH PLANT now smiles and produces from its pockets all manner of fruits which it holds in the air.]*
4TH PLANT	Get your fresh fruit here ... fruit, all sorts of fresh garden produce. Apples, oranges ... You name it, we've got it. Everything to sustain you. Come and get it, all free. *[During this last, other plants enter and accept the fruits on offer.]*
SID	*[leaving with HARRY]* Beats me why people don't use this stuff more often, Harry!

17

Waiting for God . . . Oh!

Cast:
    1ST NARRATOR
    2ND NARRATOR
    ELDERLY LADY (BETTY)
    YOUNG MAN
    YOUNG WOMAN
    STATION MASTER
    YOUTH

An ELDERLY LADY is seated to the right of centre stage, reading. At her side is a pile of books. Two or three chairs are to the left of centre stage. Two NARRATORS stand either side of the set.

1ST NARRATOR	A woman sits waiting . . .
2ND NARRATOR	. . . waiting for a train.
1ST NARRATOR	A special train on which, she has been promised, there is a place reserved for her.
2ND NARRATOR	And she has believed . . .
1ST NARRATOR	. . . She has trusted . . .
2ND NARRATOR	. . . She has faith.
1ST NARRATOR	Others come.
	[Enter left, a young couple, hand in hand.]
2ND NARRATOR	They too have heard of the special train.
1ST NARRATOR	And they wish to find out more.

YOUNG MAN	*[to BETTY]* Could you tell us something about the Golden Express please?
BETTY	The person you should ask is the Station Master. He knows more about it than I do.
YOUNG MAN	Oh right, thank you. *[Looking around]* Uh, where do we find him?
BETTY	He's not actually in today. Once a week he comes. Pops his head round the door for a little reassuring chat.
YOUNG WOMAN	When's he due in next then?
BETTY	Let's see, he was in yesterday, so it won't be for another six days I'm afraid. You could always wait. I'm sure he'd be only too happy to tell you all about the service. *[The MAN and WOMAN sit and do nothing. BETTY returns to her reading.]*
1ST NARRATOR	And so they waited . . .
2ND NARRATOR	. . . And waited . . .
1ST NARRATOR	. . . and waited . . .
2ND NARRATOR	. . . And left. *[The couple, obviously bored, exit.]*
1ST NARRATOR	And the lady didn't even notice. *[BETTY turns a page.]*
2ND NARRATOR	Eventually, the Station Master came on his weekly visit. *[The STATION MASTER enters.]*
STATION MASTER	Hello Betty, reading again are we? Carry on like this and you'll know more about the Golden Express than I do.
BETTY	*[flattered]* Get away with you, Station Master. Uh . . . *[she turns to where the couple had been seated]* . . . Oh!
STATION MASTER	What is it, Betty?
BETTY	Oh, nothing, it's just that . . . oh, it doesn't really matter.

112

STATION MASTER	Well, keep up the good work. When you've finished that reading, there's plenty more in my library to get stuck in to.
BETTY	That's very good of you, Station Master.
STATION MASTER	Goodness has nothing to do with it, my dear.
	[He exits. BETTY returns to another book.]
1ST NARRATOR	Time passed ...
2ND NARRATOR	... And another person came to ask about the Golden Express.
	[Enter a typical young 'rebel'.]
YOUTH	Is this the place to wait for the Golden Express?
BETTY	*[slightly ill at ease]* Uh, yes it is.
YOUTH	When's it due?
BETTY	Nobody knows.
YOUTH	*[sardonically]* Do what?
BETTY	Well of course, there will be indications of its arrival.
YOUTH	What, like a timetable you mean?
BETTY	Well, not exactly ... The uh, person to help you isn't really here at the moment ... *[as an afterthought]* of course, I'm sure he's not very far away.
YOUTH	Who's that, then?
BETTY	The Station Master.
YOUTH	So why can't you help me, then?
BETTY	I'm not really equipped.
YOUTH	*[pointing at the books]* What's all that, then?
BETTY	... Well, books.
YOUTH	What are they about, then?
BETTY	About? Well, they're mostly about the Golden Express.

YOUTH	How come you're not equipped, then?
BETTY	Well, I er. . . .
YOUTH	*[walking over to her]* Let's have a look at one of them. *[He takes one.]*
BETTY	*[looking nervously around her]* I'm not sure that . . .
YOUTH	*[thumbing through it]* These yours, are they?
BETTY	They're from the station library, actually. *[She stands and walks over to the door, as if in search of some help. In doing so, she reveals a big book which she has been sitting on.]*
YOUTH	*[picking it up]* This is a library book too, is it?
BETTY	No, that's mine. If you wouldn't mind. *[She takes it from him.]*
YOUTH	Expensive, is it?
BETTY	No, it just happens to mean a lot to me, that's all.
YOUTH	*[picking up another book and thumbing through it]* . . . Mean a lot to me, would it?
BETTY	Look it's not really my job to . . .
YOUTH	. . . So what is that book, then?
BETTY	It's all about the Golden Express actually.
YOUTH	And how long you been sitting on it?
BETTY	I read it every now and again.
YOUTH	You know about it, then?
BETTY	Well, yes.
YOUTH	So how come you're not equipped to tell me about it, then?
BETTY	Er . . .
YOUTH	*[pulling another chair over and placing beside hers]* Right, while we're waiting

114

for the Station Master, you can tell me
what you know. *[He sits.]*

> *[The action now freezes while the
> NARRATORS speak.]*

1ST NARRATOR | Not all will ask questions like the youth.
2ND NARRATOR | And not everyone will notice that you
are sitting on the book.

1ST NARRATOR | And if they don't?
2ND NARRATOR | Not all will catch the train.

18

Only Fools . . . !

Cast: CARETAKER
                    1ST GIRL
                    2ND GIRL
                    3RD GIRL
                    4TH GIRL

A man dressed as a CARETAKER *enters from one side of the set, just as a group of schoolgirls enters from opposite.*

1ST GIRL   Excuse me, do you look after this place?

CARETAKER   Yes.

1ST GIRL   Well uh, we're looking for the way in.

CARETAKER   This is the only entrance.

1ST GIRL   *[she makes a move forward]* Is it okay, then?

CARETAKER   *[taking a book from his pocket]* Your names?
                [The girls call out their names one by one as the CARETAKER *ticks them off. At the end of the roll call, he puts the book back in his pocket.]*
                . . . Right, well at least you're accounted for!

1ST GIRL   *[expectantly]* It's okay, then?

CARETAKER   Not to come in, it's not. I'm afraid your names are in the book of 'not allowed'.

2ND GIRL   Oh, please! We've been separated from the rest of our school party, and we're lost.

CARETAKER   Just a minute . . . *[consulting book again]* No,

117

	no. Sorry, can't help you. It was your fault, you see.
2ND GIRL	Our fault?
CARETAKER	You can't expect to come to a higher level establishment without passing the entrance examinations. Your last school told you what was expected of you.
3RD GIRL	*[militantly]* Oh, come on. That school was ever so hard on us. The place was full of antique rules.
CARETAKER	But the rules were there for your benefit, weren't they?
3RD GIRL	*[disdainfully]* Those rules were as old as the Ark . . .
CARETAKER	. . . Well, not quite . . .
3RD GIRL	. . . don't do this, don't do that. Anyone would expect us to be perfect.
CARETAKER	*[sighing]* You were certainly there to do your best, that's a sure thing.
3RD GIRL	Well, it was too hard, that's all.
CARETAKER	What happened to you all on the day of the finals?
3RD GIRL	Yes, and while we're at it, that was a bit of a dirty trick, wasn't it?
CARETAKER	How do you mean?
3RD GIRL	We weren't told the exam date, were we?
CARETAKER	*[calmly]* You were told from the very start that there was no set date for the final exam.
2ND GIRL	Do you think that's fair?
CARETAKER	I would have thought it unfair if some knew the date and others didn't. Nobody knew in fact *[emphatically]* but some were prepared . . . You haven't told me what happened that day.
3RD GIRL	We weren't there, that's all.
1ST GIRL	We'd been invited somewhere.

CARETAKER	Did you tell those in charge where you were going?
1ST GIRL	*[uncomfortably]* Not exactly, no.
3RD GIRL	Look, we just wanted a break, didn't we?
CARETAKER	So you were skiving?
3RD GIRL	What if we were?
CARETAKER	Because when the chief examiner came to the school, he couldn't find you. The girls who were there saw him coming and were prepared for the finals. They all passed and were allowed entrance here.
4TH GIRL	How do you know he couldn't find us? I don't reckon he even came looking.
CARETAKER	*[slowly]* I know, because I'm the chief examiner, and I never met you.
	[The CARETAKER slowly turns and exits. The girls exit forlornly in the other direction.]

The Dame Cecily Spume Drama Notebook

by Nick Page

AT LAST
FOR ONE BOOK ONLY!
DAME CECILY SPUME - IN PERSON

Dame Cecily Spume, *doyenne extraordinaire* of the British theatre, inventor of the Method that brought glory to Jack N., Meryl S. and Sir John G., here sets forth, for a discerning audience the tricks, knacks and wrinkles that have offered fame and fortune to generations of aspiring thespians.

Using a choice selection of eighteen profound, moving, fun-filled Christian sketches by hack scribbler Nick Page (late of Ambush Theatre Company), Dame Cecily can transform you and your drama group into the megastars you always knew you should be. 'It worked for darling Larry,' she says. 'It can work for you.'

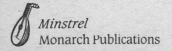
Minstrel
Monarch Publications

The Greatest Burger Ever Sold

by Nick McIvor

'Jesus, son of Joseph, was born into a working-class family in the provincial town of Nazareth.' So begins the story of the best-known character in history, and yet there are still a host of unanswered questions about his life and work. How was he treated by the press? Where did the disciples go to school? Did his miracles affect health-insurance premiums? *The Greatest Burger Ever Sold* confronts these issues.

The sketches here have appeared at universities and festivals around the country including Mayfest (Glasgow), Greenbelt (Northampton) and York. Described by *The Scotsman* at the 1983 Edinburgh Fringe as 'imaginative', 'brutal', and 'acutely observed', they relate the life of Christ through a series of eye-witnesses who were clearly implied, if not explicitly mentioned in the biblical accounts.

Would Jesus have attracted commercial sponsorship? What did Joseph's mother think? Find out in: *The Greatest Burger Ever Sold.*

NICK McIVOR is an actor, comedian and scriptwriter for stage and television. He lives in London.

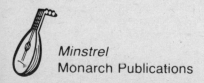

Minstrel
Monarch Publications

Clearing Away The Rubbish

by Adrian Plass

How we love to make life complicated! So much of what we do looks worth while, but unless its roots are in Reality it's just another piece of rubbish.

Through humour, poetry, songs and drama. Adrian Plass invites us to clear away the rubbish that our Infernal Enemy delights in tipping into our lives.

ADRIAN PLASS is well known for his ability to strip away the veneer of hypocrisy of super-spirituality that bedevils so many of us. Many of these pieces—ideal for amateur performance—will encourage us to rediscover an uncluttered pathway to the truth.

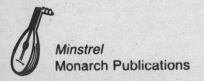

Minstrel
Monarch Publications

All Preachers Great & Small

by Peter Gammons

'A man from Leicester took his grandson to church for the first time. The lad was surprised when the collection plate came round. "You don't have to pay for me, Grandad," he whispered. "I'm not five yet."'

Many have associated religion with a serious disposition and long faces. Peter Gammons sees another side to faith. Here is a hysterical clerical collection of strange facts, stranger anecdotes and shaggy dog-collar stories: bright and sparkling, with a wry, dry twist.

Peter Gammons solemnly swears that, to the best of his knowledge, all the entries in this book are true.

'Farmer seeks lady with tractor with view to companionship and possible marriage. Send picture of tractor.'

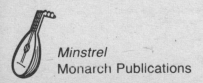

Minstrel
Monarch Publications

Monarch Publications

Monarch Publications was founded to produce books from a Christian perspective which challenge the way people think and feel. Our books are intended to appeal to a very wide constituency, in order to encourage Christian values which currently seem to be in decline.

Monarch Publications has three imprints:

<u>Monarch</u> is concerned with issues, to develop the mind.

<u>MARC</u> is a skills-based list, concentrating on leadership and mission.

<u>Minstrel</u> concentrates on creative writing, to stimulate the imagination.

Monarch Publications is owned by The Servant Trust, a Christian charity run by representatives of the evangelical church in Britain, committed to serve God in publishing and music.

For further information on the Trust, including details of how you may be able to support its work, please write to:

> The Secretary
> The Servant Trust
> 1 St Anne's Road
> Eastbourne
> East Sussex BN21 3UN
> England